MW01613187

The Gospel of Life

*Proving that Jesus Christ
is God the Savior
Coming as Life
to Propagate Himself*

Living Stream Ministry
Anaheim, California

First Edition, 1993.

ISBN 0-7363-1429-6

Published by

Living Stream Ministry
2431 W. La Palma Ave., Anaheim, CA 92801 U.S.A.
P. O. Box 2121, Anaheim, CA 92814 U.S.A.

Printed in the United States of America

02   03   04   05   06   07   08   /   10   9   8   7   6   5   4

CONTENTS

FOREWORD

The Bible is a unique book; it stands above all other books in the world. It is the world's most widely read book and has been translated into more languages than any other book.

The Bible is appreciated by millions of people for its accurate historical record, its wisdom concerning man's relationship with God and his relationship with his fellow man, and its teachings concerning ethics and morality. However, the central revelation of the Bible is life. The Bible is a book of life, and this life is a living person, the Lord Jesus Christ Himself. The Bible reveals that God desires to give eternal life to all men. This eternal life that God desires to give us is the very life of the eternal God. Since God is embodied in Jesus Christ, the life of God also is in Christ. The Bible reveals that the way for men to obtain this wonderful life is to receive Christ by believing into Him.

Among the four Gospels at the beginning of the New Testament, the Gospel of John is unique. It is the Gospel of life. The purpose of this Gospel is to show us that Jesus Christ as the eternal, divine life can meet every need of man. Man's basic need is not any material thing, nor is it to improve himself through moral teachings or religious practices. Man's basic need is to be born of God and thereby to obtain the life of God and become a son of God. According to the Gospel of John, the divine life of God regenerates us, satisfies us, heals us, enlivens us, feeds us, quenches our thirst, delivers us from the bondage of sin, opens our eyes and gives us spiritual sight, and raises us from death. Whatever our condition or situation, the life of God in Christ can meet our every need.

Our prayer is that by reading this new translation of the Gospel of John, and the two articles that follow this Gospel, you will see the very Christ revealed in this Gospel and will believe in Him and receive Him as your Redeemer, your Savior, and your life. We also pray that, after receiving Christ, you will continue to grow in the divine life by daily eating Christ as your spiritual food, drinking Christ as your spiritual drink, and breathing Christ as your spiritual breath.

THE GOSPEL ACCORDING TO
JOHN

CHAPTER 1

I. The Eternal Word Incarnated Coming to Bring God into Man
1:1—13:38

A. Introduction to Life and Building
1:1-51

1. The Word in Eternity Past, Who Was God, through Creation
Coming as Life and Light to Bring Forth the Children of God
vv. 1-13

¹ In the beginning was the Word, and the Word was with God, and the Word was God. ² He was in the beginning with God. ³ All things came into being through Him, and apart from Him not one thing came into being which has come into being. ⁴ In Him was life, and the life was the light of men. ⁵ And the light shines in the darkness, and the darkness did not overcome it. ⁶ There came a man sent from God, whose name was John. ⁷ He came for a testimony that he might testify concerning the light, that all might believe through him. ⁸ He was not the light, but *came* that he might testify concerning the light. ⁹ *This* was the true light which, coming into the world, enlightens every man. ¹⁰ He was in the world, and the world came into being through Him, yet

the world did not know Him. [11] He came to His own, yet those who were His own did not receive Him. [12] But as many as received Him, to them He gave the authority to become children of God, to those who believe into His name, [13] Who were begotten not of blood, nor of the will of the flesh, nor of the will of man, but of God.

2. The Word Becoming Flesh,
with Grace in Fullness and with Reality,
to Declare God in the Only Begotten Son of God
vv.14-18

[14] And the Word became flesh and tabernacled among us (and we beheld His glory, glory as of the only Begotten from the Father), full of grace and reality. [15] John testified concerning Him and cried out, saying, This was He of whom I said, He who is coming after me has become ahead of me, because He was before me. [16] For of His fullness we have all received, and grace upon grace. [17] For the law was given through Moses; grace and reality came through Jesus Christ. [18] No one has ever seen God; the only begotten Son, who is in the bosom of the Father, He has declared *Him*.

3. Jesus as the Lamb of God, with the Holy Spirit as the Dove,
Making the Believers Stones for the Building
of the House of God with the Son of Man
vv. 19-51

[19] And this is the testimony of John, when the Jews sent to him priests and Levites from Jerusalem to ask him, Who are you? [20] And he confessed

and did not deny, and he confessed, I am not the Christ. [21] And they asked him, What then? Are you Elijah? And he said, I am not. Are you the Prophet? And he answered, No. [22] They said then to him, Who are you, that we may give an answer to those who sent us? What do you say about yourself? [23] He said, I am a voice of one crying in the wilderness, "Make straight the way of the Lord!" as Isaiah the prophet said. [24] And those who had been sent were of the Pharisees. [25] And they asked him and said to him, Why then are you baptizing if you are not the Christ nor Elijah nor the Prophet? [26] John answered them, saying, I baptize in water; *but* among you stands One whom you do not know, [27] He who is coming after me, the thong of whose sandal I am not worthy to untie. [28] These things took place in Bethany across the Jordan, where John was baptizing.

[29] The next day he saw Jesus coming to him and said, Behold, the Lamb of God, who takes away the sin of the world! [30] This is He of whom I said, A man is coming after me who has become ahead of me, because He was before me. [31] And I did not know Him, but in order that He might be manifested to Israel, for this *reason* I came baptizing in water. [32] And John testified, saying, I beheld the Spirit descending as a dove out of heaven, and He abode upon Him. [33] And I did not know Him, but He who sent me to baptize in water, He said to me, He upon whom you see the Spirit descending and abiding upon Him, this is He who baptizes in the Holy Spirit. [34] And I have seen and have testified that this is the Son of God.

[35] Again the next day John was standing with two of his disciples, [36] And looking at Jesus walking, he said, Behold, the Lamb of God! [37] And the two disciples heard him speak *this,* and they followed Jesus. [38] And Jesus, turning and beholding them following, said to them, What are you seeking? And they said to Him, Rabbi (which translated means Teacher), where are You staying? [39] He said to them, Come, and you will see. They went therefore and saw where He was staying, and they stayed with Him that day; it was about the tenth hour. [40] One of the two who heard *this* from John and followed Him was Andrew, Simon Peter's brother. [41] He first found his own brother Simon and said to him, We have found the Messiah (which translated means Christ). [42] He led him to Jesus. Looking at him, Jesus said, You are Simon, the son of John; you shall be called Cephas (which is interpreted, Peter).

[43] The next day He wanted to go forth into Galilee, and He found Philip. And Jesus said to him, Follow Me. [44] Now Philip was from Bethsaida, of the city of Andrew and Peter. [45] Philip found Nathanael and said to him, We have found Him of whom Moses in the law, and the prophets, wrote, Jesus, the son of Joseph, from Nazareth. [46] And Nathanael said to him, Can anything good be from Nazareth? Philip said to him, Come and see. [47] Jesus saw Nathanael coming to Him and said concerning him, Behold, truly an Israelite, in whom there is no guile! [48] Nathanael said to Him, How do You know me? Jesus answered and said to him, Before Philip called

you, while you were under the fig tree, I saw you.
[49] Nathanael answered Him, Rabbi, You are the Son
of God; You are the King of Israel. [50] Jesus answered
and said to him, *Is it* because I told you that I saw
you under the fig tree *that* you believe? You shall
see greater things than these. [51] And He said to him,
Truly, truly, I say to you, You shall see heaven
opened and the angels of God ascending and descending on the Son of Man.

CHAPTER 2

B. Life's Principle and Life's Purpose
2:1-22

1. Life's Principle—To Change Death into Life
vv. 1-11

[1] And the third day a wedding took place in
Cana of Galilee, and the mother of Jesus was there.
[2] And Jesus also was invited, as well as His disciples, to the wedding.

[3] And when the wine ran out, the mother of
Jesus said to Him, They have no wine. [4] And Jesus
said to her, Woman, what do I have in this that concerns you? My hour has not yet come. [5] His mother
said to the servants, Whatever He says to you, do.
[6] Now there were six stone waterpots lying there,
according to the Jews' rite of purification, holding
two or three measures each. [7] Jesus said to them,
Fill the waterpots with water. And they filled them
up to the brim.

[8] And He said to them, Draw some out now and
take it to the master of the feast. And they took *it*

to him. [9] And when the master of the feast tasted the water which had become wine and did not know where it came from, though the servants who had drawn the water knew, the master of the feast called the bridegroom [10] And said to him, Every man sets out the good wine first, and when they have drunk freely, *then* that which is worse; you have kept the good wine until now. [11] This beginning of signs Jesus performed in Cana of Galilee and manifested His glory, and His disciples believed into Him.

2. Life's Purpose—To Build the House of God
vv. 12-22

[12] After this He went down to Capernaum, He and His mother and His brothers and His disciples; and they remained there not many days.

[13] And the Passover of the Jews was near, and Jesus went up to Jerusalem. [14] And He found in the temple those selling oxen and sheep and doves, and the moneychangers sitting *there*. [15] And having made a whip out of cords, He drove them all out of the temple, as well as the sheep and the oxen, and He poured out the money of the moneychangers and overturned their tables. [16] And to those who were selling the doves He said, Take these things away from here; do not make My Father's house a house of merchandise. [17] His disciples remembered that it was written, "The zeal of Your house shall devour Me."

[18] The Jews then answered and said to Him, What sign do you show us, seeing that you do these things? [19] Jesus answered and said to them, Destroy

this temple, and in three days I will raise it up.
[20] Then the Jews said, This temple was built in
forty-six years, and You will raise it up in three
days? [21] But He spoke of the temple of His body.
[22] When therefore He was raised from the dead, His
disciples remembered that He had said this, and
they believed the Scripture and the word which
Jesus had spoken.

C. Life Meeting the Need of Man's Every Case
2:23—11:57

1. The Need of the Moral—Life's Regenerating
2:23—3:36

[23] Now when He was in Jerusalem at the Passover, during the feast, many believed into His name
when they saw the signs which He did. [24] But Jesus
Himself did not entrust Himself to them, for He
knew all men, [25] And because He did not need anyone to testify concerning man, for He Himself knew
what was in man.

CHAPTER 3

[1] But there was a man of the Pharisees named
Nicodemus, a ruler of the Jews.
[2] This one came to Him by night and said to Him,
Rabbi, we know that You have come from God as a
teacher, for no one can do these signs that You do unless God is with him. [3] Jesus answered and said to
him, Truly, truly, I say to you, Unless one is born
anew, he cannot see the kingdom of God. [4] Nicodemus said to Him, How can a man be born when he is

old? He cannot enter a second time into his mother's womb and be born, can he? [5] Jesus answered, Truly, truly, I say to you, Unless one is born of water and the Spirit, he cannot enter into the kingdom of God. [6] That which is born of the flesh is flesh, and that which is born of the Spirit is spirit. [7] Do not marvel that I said to you, You must be born anew. [8] The wind blows where it wills, and you hear the sound of it, but you do not know where it comes from and where it goes; so is everyone who is born of the Spirit. [9] Nicodemus answered and said to Him, How can these things be? [10] Jesus answered and said to him, You are a teacher of Israel, and you do not know these things? [11] Truly, truly, I say to you, We speak that which we know and testify of that which we have seen, and yet you do not receive our testimony. [12] If I told you of the things on earth and you do not believe, how will you believe if I tell you of the things in heaven? [13] And no one has ascended into heaven, but He who descended out of heaven, the Son of Man, who is in heaven.

[14] And as Moses lifted up the serpent in the wilderness, so must the Son of Man be lifted up, [15] That every one who believes into Him may have eternal life.

[16] For God so loved the world that He gave His only begotten Son, that every one who believes into Him would not perish, but would have eternal life. [17] For God did not send the Son into the world to condemn the world, but that the world might be saved through Him. [18] He who believes into Him is not condemned; but he who does not believe has

been condemned already, because he has not believed into the name of the only begotten Son of
God.

¹⁹ And this is the condemnation, that the light
has come into the world, and men loved the darkness rather than the light, for their works were evil.
²⁰ For every one who practices evil hates the light,
and does not come to the light, lest his works be
reproved. ²¹ But he who does the truth comes to the
light, that his works may be manifested that they
are wrought in God.

²² After these things, Jesus and His disciples
came into the land of Judea, and there He spent
some time with them and baptized. ²³ And John also
was baptizing in Aenon near Salim, because there
was much water there; and people came and were
baptized; ²⁴ For John had not yet been thrown into
prison. ²⁵ There arose therefore a questioning on the
part of John's disciples with a Jew about purification. ²⁶ And they came to John and said to him,
Rabbi, He who was with you across the Jordan, of
whom you have testified, behold, He is baptizing
and all are coming to Him. ²⁷ John answered and
said, A man cannot receive anything unless it has
been given to him from heaven. ²⁸ You yourselves
testify of me that I said, I am not the Christ, but I
have been sent before Him. ²⁹ He who has the bride
is the bridegroom; but the friend of the bridegroom,
who stands and hears him, rejoices with joy because
of the bridegroom's voice. This joy of mine therefore
is made full. ³⁰ He must increase, but I *must* de-
crease.

³¹ He who comes from above is above all; he who is from the earth is of the earth and speaks out of the earth. He who comes from heaven is above all. ³² What He has seen and heard, of this He testifies, and no one receives His testimony. ³³ He who receives His testimony has sealed that God is true. ³⁴ For He whom God has sent speaks the words of God, for He gives the Spirit not by measure. ³⁵ The Father loves the Son and has given all into His hand. ³⁶ He who believes into the Son has eternal life; but he who disobeys the Son shall not see life, but the wrath of God abides upon him.

CHAPTER 4

2. The Need of the Immoral—Life's Satisfying
4:1-42

¹ When therefore the Lord knew that the Pharisees had heard that Jesus was making and baptizing more disciples than John ² (Although Jesus Himself did not baptize, but *rather* His disciples), ³ He left Judea and went away again into Galilee. ⁴ And He had to pass through Samaria. ⁵ So He came to a city of Samaria called Sychar, near the piece of land that Jacob gave to Joseph his son; ⁶ And Jacob's well was there. Jesus therefore, being wearied from the journey, sat thus by the well; it was about the sixth hour. ⁷ There came a woman of Samaria to draw water. Jesus said to her, Give Me *something* to drink. ⁸ For His disciples had gone away into the city to buy food.

⁹ The Samaritan woman then said to Him, How

is it that You, being a Jew, ask for a drink from me, who am a Samaritan woman? (For Jews have no dealings with Samaritans.) [10] Jesus answered and said to her, If you knew the gift of God and who it is who says to you, Give Me a drink, you would have asked Him, and He would have given you living water. [11] The woman said to Him, Sir, You have no bucket, and the well is deep; where then do You get this living water? [12] Are You greater than our father Jacob, who gave us the well and drank of it himself, as well as his sons and his cattle? [13] Jesus answered and said to her, Everyone who drinks of this water shall thirst again, [14] But whoever drinks of the water that I will give him shall by no means thirst forever; but the water that I will give him will become in him a spring of water gushing up into eternal life.

[15] The woman said to Him, Sir, give me this water so that I will not thirst nor come here to draw. [16] He said to her, Go, call your husband and come here. [17] The woman answered and said, I do not have a husband. Jesus said to her, You have well said, I do not have a husband, [18] For you have had five husbands, and the one you now have is not your husband; this you have said truly.

[19] The woman said to Him, Sir, I perceive that You are a prophet. [20] Our fathers worshipped in this mountain, yet you say that in Jerusalem is the place where *men* must worship. [21] Jesus said to her, Woman, believe Me, an hour is coming when neither in this mountain nor in Jerusalem will you worship the Father. [22] You worship that which you do not

know; we worship that which we know, for salvation is of the Jews. [23] But an hour is coming, and it is now, when the true worshippers will worship the Father in spirit and truthfulness, for the Father also seeks such to worship Him. [24] God is Spirit, and those who worship Him must worship in spirit and truthfulness.

[25] The woman said to Him, I know that Messiah is coming (He who is called Christ); when He comes, He will declare all things to us. [26] Jesus said to her, I, who speak to you, am *He*.

[27] And at this *point* His disciples came, and they marveled that He was speaking with a woman; yet no one said, What are You seeking? or, Why are You speaking with her? [28] Then the woman left her waterpot and went away into the city, and said to the people, [29] Come, see a man who told me all that I have done. Is this not the Christ? [30] They went out of the city and came to Him.

[31] In the meantime, the disciples urged Him, saying, Rabbi, eat. [32] But He said to them, I have food to eat that you do not know about. [33] The disciples therefore said to one another, Has anyone brought Him *anything* to eat? [34] Jesus said to them, My food is to do the will of Him who sent Me and to finish His work. [35] Do you not say that there are yet four months and then the harvest comes? Behold, I tell you, Lift up your eyes and look on the fields, for they are already white for harvest. [36] He who reaps receives wages and gathers fruit unto eternal life, in order that he who sows and he who reaps may rejoice together. [37] For in this the saying is true, One

sows and another reaps. [38] I sent you to reap that for which you have not labored; others have labored, and you have entered into their labor.

[39] And many of the Samaritans from that city believed into Him because of the word of the woman who testified, He told me all that I have done. [40] So when the Samaritans came to Him, they asked Him to remain with them, and He remained there two days. [41] And many more believed because of His word. [42] And they said to the woman, *It is* no longer because of your speaking *that* we believe, for we ourselves have heard and know that this One is truly the Savior of the world.

3. The Need of the Dying—Life's Healing
4:43-54

[43] And after the two days He went forth from there into Galilee, [44] For Jesus Himself testified that a prophet has no honor in his own country. [45] Then when He came into Galilee, the Galileans received Him, having seen all that He did in Jerusalem at the feast, for they also went to the feast.

[46] He then came again to Cana of Galilee, where He had made the water wine.

And there was a certain royal official, whose son was sick in Capernaum. [47] When he heard that Jesus had come out of Judea into Galilee, he went to Him and asked *Him* to come down and heal his son, for he was about to die. [48] Jesus therefore said to him, Unless you see signs and wonders, you will by no means believe. [49] The royal official said to Him, Sir, come down before my little child dies.

[50] Jesus said to him, Go, your son lives. The man
believed the word which Jesus said to him and went
his way. [51] And as he was now going down, his slaves
met him and said that his child was living. [52] So he
asked them the hour in which he got better. They
said then to him, Yesterday at the seventh hour the
fever left him. [53] Then the father knew that *it was* in
that hour in which Jesus said to him, Your son lives;
and he believed, he and his whole house. [54] Again,
this second sign Jesus performed when He came out
of Judea into Galilee.

CHAPTER 5

4. The Need of the Impotent—Life's Enlivening
5:1-47

[1] After these things there was a feast of the Jews,
and Jesus went up to Jerusalem. [2] Now there is in
Jerusalem near the sheepgate a pool, which is called
in Hebrew Bethesda, having five porticoes. [3] In
these lay a multitude of those who were sick, blind,
lame, *and* withered, waiting for the moving of the
water. [4] For an angel went down from time to time in
the pool and stirred up the water; the first then to
step in after the stirring up of the water was made
well of whatever disease he was being held by. [5] And
a certain man was there, who had been thirty-eight
years in his sickness. [6] When Jesus saw this one lying *there* and knew that he had already been a long
time *in that condition,* He said to him, Do you want
to get well? [7] The sick man answered Him, Sir, I
have no one to put me into the pool when the water

is stirred up; but while I am coming, another steps down before me. [8] Jesus said to him, Rise, take up your mat and walk. [9] And immediately the man became well, and he took up his mat and walked. Now it was the Sabbath on that day;

[10] Therefore the Jews said to the one who had been healed, It is the Sabbath, and it is not lawful for you to take up your mat. [11] But he answered them, He who made me well, that One said to me, Take up *your mat* and walk. [12] They asked him, Who is the man who said to you, Take up your mat and walk? [13] But he who had been healed did not know who it was, for Jesus had withdrawn, there being a crowd in that place. [14] After these things Jesus found him in the temple and said to him, Behold, you have become well; sin no more so that nothing worse happens to you. [15] The man went away and told the Jews that Jesus was the One who made him well. [16] And because of this the Jews persecuted Jesus and sought to kill Him, because He did these things on the Sabbath.

[17] But Jesus answered them, My Father is working until now, and I also am working. [18] Because of this therefore the Jews sought all the more to kill Him, because He not only broke the Sabbath but also called God His own Father, making Himself equal with God.

[19] Then Jesus answered and said to them, Truly, truly, I say to you, The Son can do nothing from Himself except what He sees the Father doing, for whatever that One does, these things the Son also does in like manner. [20] For the Father loves the Son

and shows Him all things that He Himself is doing; and greater works than these He will show Him that you may marvel. [21] For just as the Father raises the dead and gives *them* life, so also the Son gives life to whom He wills. [22] For neither does the Father judge anyone, but He has given all judgment to the Son, [23] In order that all may honor the Son even as they honor the Father. He who does not honor the Son does not honor the Father who sent Him. [24] Truly, truly, I say to you, He who hears My word and believes Him who sent Me has eternal life, and does not come into judgment but has passed out of death into life. [25] Truly, truly, I say to you, An hour is coming, and it is now, when the dead will hear the voice of the Son of God, and those who hear will live. [26] For just as the Father has life in Himself, so He gave to the Son to also have life in Himself; [27] And He gave Him authority to execute judgment because He is the Son of Man. [28] Do not marvel at this, for an hour is coming in which all in the tombs will hear His voice [29] And will come forth: those who have done good, to the resurrection of life; and those who have practiced evil, to the resurrection of judgment.

[30] I can do nothing from Myself; as I hear, I judge, and My judgment is just, because I do not seek My own will but the will of Him who sent Me.

[31] If I testify concerning Myself, My testimony is not true.

[32] There is another who testifies concerning Me, and I know that the testimony which he testifies concerning Me is true. [33] You have sent *people* to

John, and he has testified to the truth. [34] But *it is* not from man *that* I receive My testimony, but I say these things that you may be saved. [35] He was the lamp that was burning and shining, and you were willing to exult for a while in his light.

[36] But I have the testimony *which is* greater than *that* of John, for the works which the Father has given Me to finish, the works themselves which I do, testify concerning Me that the Father has sent Me.

[37] And the Father who sent Me, He has testified concerning Me. You have neither heard His voice at any time, nor have you seen His form, [38] And you do not have His word abiding in you, for Him whom He sent, this One you do not believe.

[39] You search the Scriptures, because you think that in them you have eternal life; and it is these that testify concerning Me. [40] Yet you are not willing to come to Me that you may have life. [41] I do not receive glory from men. [42] But I know you, that you do not have the love of God in yourselves. [43] I have come in the name of My Father, and you do not receive Me; if another comes in his own name, you will receive him. [44] How can you believe when you receive glory from one another and do not seek the glory that is from the only God? [45] Do not think that I will accuse you before the Father; there is one who accuses you: Moses, in whom you have set your hope. [46] For if you believed Moses, you would believe Me; for he wrote concerning Me. [47] But if you do not believe his writings, how will you believe My words?

CHAPTER 6

5. The Need of the Hungry—Life's Feeding
6:1-71

[1] After these things Jesus went away across the Sea of Galilee, *which is the Sea* of Tiberias. [2] And a great crowd followed Him, because they saw the signs which He did on those who were sick. [3] And Jesus went up to the mountain and sat there with His disciples. [4] Now the Passover, the feast of the Jews, was near. [5] Jesus then lifting up His eyes and seeing that a great crowd was coming toward Him, said to Philip, Where shall we buy bread that these may eat? [6] But this He said to test him, for He Himself knew what He was about to do. [7] Philip answered Him, Two hundred denarii worth of bread is not sufficient for them, that each one may take a little. [8] One of His disciples, Andrew, Simon Peter's brother, said to Him, [9] There is a little boy here who has five barley loaves and two fish; but what are these for so many? [10] Jesus said, Have the people recline. Now there was much grass in the place. So the men reclined, in number about five thousand. [11] Jesus then took the loaves, and when He had given thanks, He distributed to those who were reclining; likewise also of the fish, as much as they wanted. [12] And when they were filled, He said to His disciples, Gather the broken pieces leftover that nothing may be lost. [13] So they gathered *them* and filled twelve handbaskets with broken pieces from the five barley loaves which were left over among those who had eaten. [14] The

people therefore, seeing the sign which He did, said, This is truly the Prophet who is to come into the world.

[15] Then Jesus, knowing that they were about to come and take *Him* by force to make Him King, withdrew again to the mountain, Himself alone.

[16] And when evening fell, His disciples went down to the sea, [17] And they got into a boat and began crossing the sea to Capernaum. And it had already become dark, and Jesus had not yet come to them. [18] And because a strong wind was blowing, the sea was churning. [19] Then, when they had rowed about twenty-five or thirty stadia, they saw Jesus walking on the sea and coming near the boat, and they became frightened. [20] But He said to them, It is I. Do not be afraid. [21] Then they were willing to take Him into the boat; and immediately the boat was at the land to which they were going.

[22] The next day the crowd which stood on the other side of the sea saw that there had been no other small boat there except one, and that Jesus had not gotten into the boat with His disciples, but *that* His disciples had gone away alone. [23] But other small boats from Tiberias came near to the place where they ate the bread after the Lord had given thanks. [24] So when the crowd saw that Jesus was not there, nor His disciples, they themselves got into the small boats and came to Capernaum, seeking Jesus. [25] And when they found Him on the other side of the sea, they said to Him, Rabbi, when did You get here? [26] Jesus answered them and said, Truly, truly, I say to you, You seek Me not because

you have seen signs, but because you ate of the bread and were filled. [27] Work not for the food which perishes, but for the food which abides unto eternal life, which the Son of Man will give you; for Him has the Father, *even* God, sealed. [28] Then they said to Him, What shall we do that we may work the works of God? [29] Jesus answered and said to them, This is the work of God, that you believe into Him whom He has sent. [30] They said then to Him, What sign then will You do that we may see and believe You? What work will You do? [31] Our fathers ate the manna in the wilderness, as it is written, "He gave them bread out of heaven to eat."

[32] Jesus therefore said to them, Truly, truly, I say to you, Moses has not given you the bread out of heaven, but My Father gives you the true bread out of heaven. [33] For the bread of God is He who comes down out of heaven and gives life to the world. [34] They said therefore to Him, Lord, give us this bread always. [35] Jesus said to them, I am the bread of life; he who comes to Me shall by no means hunger, and he who believes into Me shall by no means ever thirst. [36] But I have said to you that you have also seen Me, and yet you do not believe. [37] All that the Father gives Me will come to Me, and him who comes to Me I shall by no means cast out. [38] For I have come down from heaven not to do My own will but the will of Him who sent Me. [39] And this is the will of Him who sent Me, that of all which He has given Me I should lose nothing but should raise it up in the last day. [40] For this is the will of My Father, that every one who beholds the Son and

believes into Him should have eternal life, and I will raise him up in the last day.

[41] The Jews therefore murmured concerning Him because He said, I am the bread that came down out of heaven. [42] And they said, Is not this Jesus, the son of Joseph, whose father and mother we know? How does He now say, I have come down out of heaven? [43] Jesus answered and said unto them, Do not murmur among yourselves. [44] No one can come to Me unless the Father who sent Me draws him; and I will raise him up in the last day. [45] It is written in the prophets, "And they shall all be taught of God." Every one who has heard and learned from the Father comes to Me. [46] Not that anyone has seen the Father, except Him who is from God, He has seen the Father. [47] Truly, truly, I say to you, He who believes has eternal life. [48] I am the bread of life. [49] Your fathers ate the manna in the wilderness, and they died. [50] This is the bread which comes down out of heaven, that anyone may eat of it and not die. [51] I am the living bread which came down out of heaven; if anyone eats of this bread, he shall live forever; And the bread which I will give is My flesh, *given* for the life of the world.

[52] The Jews then contended with one another, saying, How can this man give us His flesh to eat? [53] Jesus therefore said to them, Truly, truly, I say to you, Unless you eat the flesh of the Son of Man and drink His blood, you do not have life within yourselves. [54] He who eats My flesh and drinks My blood has eternal life, and I will raise him up in the last

day. [55] For My flesh is true food, and My blood is true drink.

[56] He who eats My flesh and drinks My blood abides in Me and I in him. [57] As the living Father has sent Me and I live because of the Father, so he who eats Me, he also shall live because of Me. [58] This is the bread which came down out of heaven, not as the fathers ate and died; he who eats this bread shall live forever. [59] He said these things in a synagogue as He taught in Capernaum.

[60] Many therefore of His disciples, when they heard *this*, said, This word is hard; who can hear it? [61] But Jesus, knowing in Himself that His disciples were murmuring about this, said to them, Does this stumble you? [62] Then what if you saw the Son of Man ascending to where He was before?

[63] It is the Spirit who gives life; the flesh profits nothing; the words which I have spoken to you are spirit and are life. [64] But there are some of you who do not believe. For Jesus knew from the beginning who were the ones who did not believe and who was the one who would betray Him. [65] And He said, For this *reason* I have told you that no one can come to Me unless it has been given to him from the Father.

[66] From that time many of His disciples went back to what *they left* behind and no longer walked with Him. [67] Jesus therefore said to the twelve, Do you also want to go away? [68] Simon Peter answered Him, Lord, to whom shall we go? You have words of eternal life, [69] And we have believed and have come to know that You are the Holy One of God. [70] Jesus answered them, *Was it* not I *who* chose you, the

twelve? Yet one of you is a devil. [71] Now He spoke of Judas, *the son* of Simon Iscariot, for he, one of the twelve, would betray Him.

CHAPTER 7

6. The Need of the Thirsty—Life's Quenching
7:1-52

[1] And after these things Jesus walked in Galilee, for He would not walk in Judea, because the Jews were seeking to kill Him. [2] Now the Jews' Feast of Tabernacles was near.

[3] His brothers therefore said to Him, Depart from here and go into Judea, so that Your disciples also may behold Your works which You are doing; [4] For no one does anything in secret and himself seeks to be *known* openly. If You do these things, manifest Yourself to the world. [5] For not even His brothers believed into Him.

[6] Jesus therefore said to them, My time has not yet come, but your time is always ready. [7] The world cannot hate you, but it hates Me, because I testify concerning it, that its works are evil. [8] You go up to the feast; I am not going up to this feast, because My time has not yet been fulfilled. [9] And having said these things to them, He remained in Galilee.

[10] But when His brothers had gone up to the feast, then He Himself also went up, not openly, but as *it were* in secret. [11] The Jews therefore sought Him at the feast and said, Where is He? [12] And there was much murmuring about Him

among the crowds: some said, He is a good man;
but others said, No; rather He leads the crowd
astray. [13] Yet no one spoke openly about Him for
fear of the Jews.

[14] But when it was now the middle of the feast,
Jesus went up into the temple and began to teach.
[15] The Jews therefore marveled and said, How does
this man know letters, without ever having stud-
ied? [16] Jesus therefore answered them and said,
My teaching is not Mine, but His who sent Me. [17] If
anyone resolves to do His will, he will know concerning the teaching, whether it is of God or
whether I speak from Myself. [18] He who speaks
from himself seeks his own glory; but He who
seeks the glory of Him who sent Him, this One is
true, and unrighteousness is not in Him. [19] Has not
Moses given you the law? Yet none of you keeps the
law. Why do you seek to kill Me? [20] The crowd answered, You have a demon! Who is seeking to kill
You? [21] Jesus answered and said to them, I did one
work, and you all marvel. [22] For the same reason
Moses gave you circumcision (not that it is from
Moses, but from the fathers), and on the Sabbath
you circumcise a man. [23] If a man receives circumcision on the Sabbath that the law of Moses may
not be broken, are you angry with Me because
I made an entire man well on the Sabbath? [24] Do
not judge according to appearance, but judge the
righteous judgment.

[25] Then some of the people of Jerusalem said, Is
not this the One whom they are seeking to kill?
[26] And look, He is speaking openly, and they say

nothing to Him. Have the rulers, perhaps, really recognized that this is the Christ? [27] But we know where this man is from; yet when the Christ comes, no one knows where He is from. [28] Jesus therefore cried out in the temple, teaching and saying, You both know Me and know where I am from; and I have not come of Myself, but He who sent Me is true, whom you do not know. [29] I know Him, because I am from Him, and He sent Me. [30] They sought then to seize Him, yet no one laid a hand on Him, because His hour had not yet come. [31] But many out of the crowd believed into Him and said, Will the Christ, when He comes, do more signs than this man has done? [32] The Pharisees heard the crowd murmuring these things about Him, and the chief priests and the Pharisees sent attendants to arrest Him. [33] Jesus therefore said, I am still with you a little while, and *then* I am going to Him who sent Me. [34] You will seek Me and will not find Me; and where I am, you cannot come. [35] The Jews then said to one another, Where is this man about to go that we will not find Him? Is He about to go to the *Jews in* dispersion among the Greeks and teach the Greeks? [36] What is the word which He said, You will seek Me and will not find Me; and where I am, you cannot come?

[37] Now on the last day, the great *day* of the feast, Jesus stood and cried out, saying, If anyone thirsts, let him come to Me and drink. [38] He who believes into Me, as the Scripture said, out of his innermost being shall flow rivers of living water. [39] But this He said concerning the Spirit, whom those who

believed into Him were about to receive; for *the* Spirit was not yet, because Jesus had not yet been glorified.

[40] *Some* of the crowd therefore, when they heard these words, said, This is truly the Prophet. [41] Others said, This is the Christ. But some said, Does then the Christ come out of Galilee? [42] Has not the Scripture said that the Christ comes out of the seed of David and from Bethlehem, the village where David was? [43] So there arose a division among the crowd because of Him. [44] And some of them wanted to seize Him, but no one laid hands on Him.

[45] The attendants therefore came to the chief priests and Pharisees, and these said to them, Why did you not bring Him? [46] The attendants answered, Never has a man spoken as this man *has*. [47] The Pharisees then answered them, Have you also been deceived? [48] Has any one of the rulers or Pharisees believed into Him? [49] But this crowd which does not know the law is accursed. [50] Nicodemus said to them (he who came to Him before, being one of them), [51] Does our law condemn a man unless it first hears from him and knows what he is doing? [52] They answered and said to him, Are you also from Galilee? Search and see that no prophet arises out of Galilee.

7. The Need of Those under the Bondage of Sin— Life's Setting Free
7:53—8:59

[53] And everyone went to his *own* house.

CHAPTER 8

[1] But Jesus went to the Mount of Olives. [2] And early in the morning He came again into the temple, and all the people came to Him, and He sat down and taught them. [3] And the scribes and Pharisees brought a woman caught in adultery, and having set her in the midst, [4] They said to Him, Teacher, this woman has been caught committing adultery, in the very act. [5] Now in the law, Moses commanded us to stone such women. What then do you say? [6] But they said this to tempt Him, so that they might have *reason* to accuse Him. But Jesus stooped down and wrote with His finger on the ground. [7] But when they persisted in questioning Him, He stood up and said to them, He who is without sin among you, let him *be the* first to throw a stone at her. [8] And again He stooped down and wrote on the ground. [9] And when they heard *that,* they went out one by one, beginning with the older ones. And Jesus was left alone, and the woman *stood* where she was, in the midst.

[10] And Jesus stood up and said to her, Woman, where are they? Has no one condemned you? [11] And she said, No one, Lord. And Jesus said, Neither do I condemn you; go, and from now on sin no more.

[12] Again therefore Jesus spoke to them, saying, I am the light of the world; he who follows Me shall by no means walk in darkness, but shall have the light of life. [13] The Pharisees then said to Him, You are testifying concerning Yourself; Your testimony is not true. [14] Jesus answered and said to them, Even if I testify concerning Myself, My testimony

is true, for I know where I came from and where I am going; but you do not know where I come from or where I am going. [15] You judge according to the flesh; I judge no one. [16] But even if I do judge, My judgment is true, for I am not alone, but I and the Father who sent Me. [17] And in your law also it has been written that the testimony of two men is true: [18] I am One who testifies concerning Myself, and the Father who sent Me testifies concerning Me. [19] They said then to Him, Where is Your Father? Jesus answered. You know neither Me nor My Father; if you knew Me, you would know My Father also. [20] These words He spoke in the treasury as He taught in the temple; and no one seized Him, because His hour had not yet come.

[21] He said therefore again to them, I am going away, and you will seek Me and will die in your sin. Where I am going, you cannot come. [22] The Jews then said, He is not going to kill Himself, is He, for He says, Where I am going, you cannot come? [23] And He said to them, You are from below, I am from above; you are of this world, I am not of this world. [24] Therefore I said to you that you will die in your sins; for unless you believe that I am, you will die in your sins. [25] They said then to Him, Who are You? Jesus said to them, Altogether that which I also tell you. [26] I have many things to say and to judge concerning you, but He who sent Me is true, and what I have heard from Him, these things I speak to the world. [27] They did not understand that He was speaking to them of the Father.

[28] Jesus therefore said to them, When you lift up

the Son of Man, then you will know that I am, and *that* I do nothing from Myself, but as My Father has taught Me, I speak these things. [29] And He who sent Me is with Me; He has not left Me alone, for I always do the things that are pleasing to Him. [30] As He spoke these things, many believed into Him.

[31] Then Jesus said to those Jews who believed Him, If you abide in My word, you are truly My disciples; [32] And you shall know the truth, and the truth shall set you free. [33] They answered Him, We are Abraham's seed and have never yet been enslaved to anyone. How *is it that* You say, You shall become free? [34] Jesus answered them, Truly, truly, I say to you, Everyone who commits sin is a slave of sin. [35] And the slave does not abide in the house forever; the son does abide forever. [36] If therefore the Son sets you free, you shall be free indeed.

[37] I know that you are Abraham's seed; but you seek to kill Me because My word has no place in you. [38] I speak the things which I have seen with My Father; so then, you also do the things which you have heard from your father. [39] They answered and said to Him, Our father is Abraham. Jesus said to them, If you were Abraham's children, you would do the works of Abraham. [40] But now you are seeking to kill Me, a man who has told you the truth which I heard from God; Abraham did not do this. [41] You do the works of your father. They then said to Him, We were not born of fornication; we have one Father, God. [42] Jesus said to them, If God were your Father you would love Me; for I came forth out from God

and have come *from Him*; for I have not come of
Myself, but He sent Me. [43] Why do you not understand My speaking? *It is* because you cannot hear
My word. [44] You are *of your* father the devil, and you
want to do the desires of your father. He was a mur-
derer from the beginning and does not stand in the
truth, because there is no truth in him. When he
speaks the lie, he speaks *it* out of his own *posses-
sions*; for he is a liar and the father of it.

[45] But because I speak the truth, you do not
believe Me. [46] Which of you convicts Me of sin?
Since I speak truth, why do you not believe Me?
[47] He who is of God hears the words of God; for this
reason you do not hear *them,* because you are not of
God. [48] The Jews answered and said to Him, Have
we not spoken well *in saying* that You are a Samaritan and have a demon? [49] Jesus answered, I do not
have a demon, but I honor My Father, and you dis-
honor Me. [50] But I do not seek My glory; there is
One who seeks *glory for Me* and judges. [51] Truly,
truly, I say to you, If anyone keeps My word, he
shall by no means see death forever.

[52] The Jews therefore said to Him, Now we know
that You have a demon. Abraham died, and the
prophets *too;* yet You say, If anyone keeps My word,
he shall by no means taste death forever. [53] Are You
greater than our father Abraham, who died? The
prophets died too. Who are You making Yourself?
[54] Jesus answered, If I glorify Myself, My glory is
nothing; it is My Father who glorifies Me, of whom
you say that He is your God. [55] Yet you have not
known Him, but I know Him. And if I say that I do

not know Him, I will be like you, a liar; but I do know Him and I keep His word. [56] Your father Abraham exulted that he would see My day, and he saw *it* and rejoiced. [57] The Jews then said to Him, You are not yet fifty years old, and have You seen Abraham? [58] Jesus said to them, Truly, truly, I say to you, Before Abraham came into being, I am. [59] So they picked up stones to throw at Him, but Jesus was hidden and went out of the temple.

CHAPTER 9

8. The Need of the Blind in Religion—
Life's Sight and Life's Shepherding
9:1—10:42

[1] And as He passed by, He saw a man blind from birth. [2] And His disciples asked Him, saying, Rabbi, who sinned, this man or his parents, that he would be born blind? [3] Jesus answered, Neither has this man sinned nor his parents, *but he was born so,* that the works of God might be manifested in him.

[4] We must work the works of Him who sent Me while it is day; night is coming when no one can work. [5] While I am in the world, I am the light of the world. [6] When He had said this, He spat on the ground and made clay of the spittle and anointed his eyes with the clay, [7] And He said to him, Go, wash in the pool of Siloam (which is interpreted, Sent). He went therefore and washed and came *away* seeing. [8] The neighbors then and those who previously saw him as a beggar said, Is not this the one who used to sit and beg? [9] Some said, This is he.

Others said, No, but he is like him. He said, I am *the one*. [10] They said then to him, How then were your eyes opened? [11] He answered, The man called Jesus made clay and anointed my eyes, and said to me, Go to the *pool* of Siloam and wash. I went therefore and washed, and I received my sight. [12] And they said to him, Where is He? He said, I do not know. [13] They brought him who was once blind to the Pharisees.

[14] Now it was the Sabbath, on which day Jesus made the clay and opened his eyes. [15] Again therefore the Pharisees also asked him how he received his sight. And he said to them, He put clay on my eyes, and I washed, and I see. [16] Then some of the Pharisees said, This man is not from God, because He does not keep the Sabbath. But others said, How can a man *who is* a sinner do such signs? And there was a division among them. [17] Then they said to the blind man again, What do you say about Him, in that He opened your eyes? And he said, He is a prophet. [18] The Jews then did not believe concerning him that he had been blind and had received his sight, until they called the parents of him who had received his sight [19] And asked them, saying, Is this your son, of whom you say that he was born blind? How then does he now see? [20] Then his parents answered *them* and said, We know that this is our son and that he was born blind. [21] But how he now sees, we do not know; or who opened his eyes, we do not know. Ask him; he is of age; he will speak for himself. [22] His parents said these things because they feared the Jews, for the Jews

had already agreed that if anyone confessed Him *to be the* Christ, he should be put out of the synagogue. [23] Because of this his parents said, He is of age; question him. [24] Therefore a second time they called the man who had been blind, and said to him, Give glory to God; we know that this man is a sinner. [25] Then he answered, Whether *or not* He is a sinner, I do not know; one thing I do know, that though I was blind, now I see. [26] They said then to him, What did He do to you? How did He open your eyes? [27] He answered them, I told you already and you did not hear. Why do you want to hear *it* again? Do you also want to become His disciples? [28] And they reviled him and said, You are His disciple; but we are disciples of Moses. [29] We know that God has spoken to Moses, but as for this man, we do not know where He is from. [30] The man answered and said to them, Why here is an amazing thing, that you do not know where He is from, and *yet* He opened my eyes! [31] We know that God does not hear sinners, but if anyone is God-fearing and does His will, He hears him. [32] Since time began it has never been heard that anyone opened the eyes of one born blind. [33] If this man were not from God, He could do nothing. [34] They answered and said to him, You were wholly born in sins, and you are teaching us? And they cast him out.

[35] Jesus heard that they had cast him out, and He found him and said, Do you believe into the Son of God? [36] He answered and said, And who is He, Lord, that I may believe into Him? [37] Jesus said to him, You have both seen Him, and He is the One

speaking with you. [38] And he said, Lord, I believe; and he worshipped Him.

[39] And Jesus said, For judgment I have come into this world, that those who do not see may see, and that those who see may become blind. [40] *Some* of the Pharisees who were with Him heard these things and said to Him, We are not blind also, are we? [41] Jesus said to them, If you were blind, you would not have sin; but now *that* you say, We see; your sin remains.

CHAPTER 10

[1] Truly, truly, I say to you, He who does not enter through the door into the sheepfold, but climbs up from somewhere else, he is a thief and a robber; [2] But he who enters through the door is the shepherd of the sheep. [3] To him the doorkeeper opens, and the sheep hear his voice; and he calls his own sheep by name and leads them out. [4] When he puts forth all his own, he goes before them, and the sheep follow him because they know his voice. [5] But they will by no means follow a stranger, but will flee from him, because they do not know the voice of strangers. [6] This parable Jesus spoke to them, but they did not know what those things meant that He spoke to them.

[7] Jesus therefore said to them again, Truly, truly, I say to you that I am the door of the sheep. [8] All who came before Me are thieves and robbers, but the sheep did not hear them. [9] I am the door; if anyone enters through Me, he shall be saved and shall go in and go out and shall find pasture.

[10] The thief does not come except to steal and kill and destroy; I have come that they may have life and may have *it* abundantly. [11] I am the good Shepherd; the good Shepherd lays down His life for the sheep. [12] He who is a hireling and not the shepherd, whose own the sheep are not, sees the wolf coming and leaves the sheep and flees; and the wolf snatches them and scatters *them.* [13] *He flees* because he is a hireling and it does not matter to him concerning the sheep. [14] I am the good Shepherd, and I know My own, and My own know Me, [15] Even as the Father knows Me and I know the Father; and I lay down My life for the sheep. [16] And I have other sheep, which are not of this fold; I must lead them also, and they shall hear My voice, and there shall be one flock, one Shepherd. [17] For this *reason* the Father loves Me, because I lay down My life that I may take it again. [18] No one takes it away from Me, but I lay it down of Myself. I have authority to lay it down, and I have authority to take it again. This commandment I received from My Father.

[19] A division again took place among the Jews because of these words. [20] And many of them said, He has a demon and is insane. Why do you listen to Him? [21] Others said, These are not the words of one *who is* demon possessed. Can a demon open the eyes of the blind?

[22] At that time the Feast of the Dedication occurred in Jerusalem, *and* it was winter. [23] And Jesus was walking in the temple in the portico of Solomon. [24] The Jews therefore surrounded Him and said to Him, How long will You hold our soul in suspense? If

You are the Christ, tell us plainly. [25] Jesus answered them, I told you, and you do not believe. The works which I do in My Father's name, these testify concerning Me; [26] But you do not believe, because you are not of My sheep. [27] My sheep hear My voice, and I know them, and they follow Me; [28] And I give to them eternal life, and they shall by no means perish forever, and no one shall snatch them out of My hand. [29] My Father, who has given *them* to Me, is greater than all, and no one can snatch *them* out of My Father's hand. [30] I and the Father are one.

[31] The Jews again took up stones that they might stone Him. [32] Jesus answered them, I have shown you many good works from the Father; for which of these works are you stoning Me? [33] The Jews answered Him, We are not stoning You for a good work, but for blasphemy, and because You, being a man, are making Yourself God. [34] Jesus answered them, Is it not written in your law, "I said, You are gods"? [35] If He said they *were* gods, to whom the word of God came, and the Scripture cannot be broken, [36] Do you say of Him whom the Father has sanctified and sent into the world, You are blaspheming, because I said, I am the Son of God? [37] If I do not do the works of My Father, do not believe Me; [38] But if I do *them,* even if you do not believe Me, believe the works so that you may come to know and continue to know that the Father *is* in Me and I *am* in the Father. [39] Then they sought again to seize Him, yet He went forth out of their hand.

[40] And He went away again across the Jordan, to the place where John was baptizing at first, and He

remained there. [41] And many came to Him and said, John did no sign, but all the things John said concerning this man were true. [42] And many believed into Him there.

CHAPTER 11

9. The Need of the Dead—Life's Resurrecting
11:1-57

[1] Now there was a certain man who was sick, Lazarus from Bethany, of the village of Mary and her sister Martha. [2] It was *that* Mary who anointed the Lord with ointment and wiped His feet with her hair, whose brother Lazarus was sick. [3] The sisters therefore sent to Him saying, Lord, behold, *he* whom You love is sick. [4] But when Jesus heard *it,* He said, This sickness is not unto death, but for the glory of God, in order that the Son of God may be glorified through it.

[5] Now Jesus loved Martha and her sister and Lazarus. [6] When therefore He heard that he was sick, He remained at that time in the place where He was for two days. [7] Then after this He said to the disciples, Let us go into Judea again. [8] The disciples said to Him, Rabbi, the Jews were just now seeking to stone You, and You are going there again? [9] Jesus answered, Are there not twelve hours in the day? If anyone walks in the day, he does not stumble, because he sees the light of this world. [10] But if anyone walks in the night, he stumbles, because the light is not in him. [11] He said these things, and after this He said to them, Our

friend Lazarus has fallen asleep; but I am going that I may wake him out of sleep. [12] The disciples then said to Him, Lord, if he has fallen asleep, he will recover. [13] But Jesus had spoken about his death, but they thought that He was speaking about taking rest in sleep. [14] So Jesus then told them plainly, Lazarus has died. [15] And I rejoice for your sakes that I was not there, so that you may believe; but let us go to him. [16] Then Thomas, who is called Didymus, said to his fellow disciples, Let us also go, that we may die with Him.

[17] Then when Jesus came, He found that he had already been in the tomb four days. [18] Now Bethany was near Jerusalem, about fifteen stadia away. [19] And many of the Jews had come to Martha and Mary to console them concerning their brother. [20] Martha therefore, when she heard that Jesus was coming, went to meet Him; but Mary sat in the house. [21] Then Martha said to Jesus, Lord, if You had been here, my brother would not have died. [22] But even now I know that whatever You ask of God, God will give You. [23] Jesus said to her, Your brother will rise again. [24] Martha said to Him, I know that he will rise again in the resurrection in the last day. [25] Jesus said to her, I am the resurrection and the life; hc who believes into Me, even if he should die, shall live; [26] And every one who lives and believes into Me shall by no means die forever. Do you believe this? [27] She said to Him, Yes, Lord; I have believed that You are the Christ, the Son of God, He who comes into the world. [28] And when she had said this, she went away and called Mary her

sister secretly, saying, The Teacher is here and is calling you. ²⁹ And she, when she heard *this,* rose quickly and came to Him. ³⁰ Now Jesus had not yet come into the village, but was still in the place where Martha met Him. ³¹ The Jews then who were with her in the house and were consoling her, when they saw that Mary rose up quickly and went out, followed her, supposing that she was going to the tomb to weep there. ³² Then Mary, when she came to where Jesus was, saw Him and fell at His feet, saying to Him, Lord, if You had been here, my brother would not have died. ³³ Then Jesus, when He saw her weeping and the Jews who came with her weeping, was moved with indignation in His spirit and was troubled, ³⁴ And He said, Where have you put him? They said to Him, Lord, come and see. ³⁵ Jesus wept. ³⁶ The Jews then said, Behold how He loved him! ³⁷ But some of them said, Could not He who opened the eyes of the blind man also have caused that this man would not die? ³⁸ Jesus therefore, moved with indignation again in Himself, came to the tomb. Now it was a cave, and a stone was lying against it. ³⁹ Jesus said, Take away the stone. Martha, the sister of him who was deceased, said to Him, Lord, by now he smells, for *it is* the fourth day *that* he is *there.* ⁴⁰ Jesus said to her, Did I not tell you that if you believe you will see the glory of God?

⁴¹ Then they took the stone away. And Jesus lifted up His eyes and said, Father, I thank You that You have heard Me. ⁴² And I knew that You always hear Me; but because of the crowd standing around,

I said *it,* that they may believe that You have sent Me. [43] And when He had said these things, He cried out with a loud voice, Lazarus, come out! [44] And he who had died came out, bound hand and foot with cloths, and his face was bound about with a handkerchief. Jesus said to them, Loose him and let him go.

[45] Many of the Jews therefore who had come to Mary and beheld the things that He did believed into Him. [46] But some of them went away to the Pharisees and told them the things that Jesus did.

[47] Then the chief priests and the Pharisees assembled a council and said, What do we do? For this man is doing many signs. [48] If we let Him do so, all will believe into Him, and the Romans will come and take away both our place and *our* nation. [49] But a certain one of them, Caiaphas, who was high priest that year, said to them, You know nothing at all, [50] Nor do you take account *of the fact* that it is expedient for you that one man die for the people and *that* not the whole nation perish. [51] But this he did not say from himself, but being high priest that year, he prophesied that Jesus was to die for the nation, [52] And not for the nation only, but that He might also gather into one the children of God who are scattered abroad. [53] From that day therefore they took counsel to kill Him.

[54] Jesus therefore no longer walked openly among the Jews, but went away from there to the region near the wilderness, into a city called Ephraim, and there He remained with the disciples. [55] Now the Passover of the Jews was near, and many went up

to Jerusalem out of the country before the Passover in order to purify themselves. [56] They then sought Jesus, and said to one another as they stood in the temple, What do you think? That He will not, by any means, come to the feast? [57] Now the chief priests and the Pharisees had given orders that if anyone knew where He was, he should disclose it, so that they might arrest Him.

CHAPTER 12

D. Life's Issue and Multiplication
12:1-50

1. Life's Issue—A House of Feasting
(a Miniature of the Church Life)
vv. 1-11

[1] Then Jesus, six days before the Passover, came to Bethany, where Lazarus was, whom Jesus had raised from the dead. [2] Therefore they made Him a supper there; and Martha served, but Lazarus was one of the ones reclining *at table* with Him. [3] Then Mary took a pound of ointment, of very valuable pure nard, and anointed the feet of Jesus, and wiped His feet with her hair; and the house was filled with the fragrance of the ointment. [4] But Judas Iscariot, one of His disciples, who was about to betray Him, said, [5] Why was this ointment not sold for three hundred denarii and given to the poor? [6] But he said this not because it mattered to him concerning the poor, but because he was a thief, and holding the purse, carried off what was put into *it*. [7] Then Jesus said, Leave her alone; she has

reserved it for the day of My burial. ⁸ For the poor
you always have with you, but you do not always
have Me. ⁹ Then a great crowd of the Jews found
out that He was there, and they came, not because
of Jesus only, but that they might also see Lazarus,
whom He had raised from the dead. ¹⁰ And the chief
priests took counsel to kill Lazarus also, ¹¹ Because
on account of him many of the Jews went away and
believed into Jesus.

2. Life's Multiplication for the Church
through Death and Resurrection (the Glorification of God
and the Judgment upon the World and Satan Implied)
vv. 12-36a

¹² On the next day, the great crowd who had come
to the feast, when they heard that Jesus was coming into Jerusalem, ¹³ Took the branches of the
palm trees and went out to meet Him, and cried out,
Hosanna! Blessed is He who comes in the name of
the Lord, even the King of Israel! ¹⁴ And Jesus, having found a young donkey, sat on it, as it is written,
¹⁵ "Fear not, daughter of Zion; behold, your King
comes, sitting on a donkey's colt." ¹⁶ These things
His disciples did not understand at first, but when
Jesus was glorified, then they remembered that
these things were written of Him and *that* they had
done these things to Him. ¹⁷ The crowd therefore
that was with Him when He called Lazarus out of
the tomb and raised him from the dead testified.
¹⁸ For this *reason* the crowd also went and met Him,
because they heard that He had done this sign.
¹⁹ The Pharisees then said to one another, You see

that you are not doing anything worthwhile; behold, the world has gone after Him.

²⁰ And there were some Greeks among those who went up to worship at the feast. ²¹ These then came to Philip, who was from Bethsaida of Galilee, and asked him, saying, Sir, we wish to see Jesus. ²² Philip came and told Andrew; Andrew came, and Philip *too,* and they told Jesus. ²³ And Jesus answered them, saying, The hour has come for the Son of Man to be glorified. ²⁴ Truly, truly, I say to you, Unless the grain of wheat falls into the ground and dies, it abides alone; but if it dies, it bears much fruit. ²⁵ He who loves his soul-life loses it; and he who hates his soul-life in this world shall keep it unto eternal life. ²⁶ If anyone serves Me, let him follow Me; and where I am, there also My servant will be. If anyone serves Me, the Father will honor him. ²⁷ Now is My soul troubled; and what shall I say? Father, save Me out of this hour. But for this *reason* I have come to this hour. ²⁸ Father, glorify Your name. Then a voice came out of heaven: I have both glorified *it* and will glorify *it* again. ²⁹ The crowd therefore which stood by and heard *it* said that there had been thunder; others said, An angel has spoken to Him. ³⁰ Jesus answered and said, This voice has not come for My sake, but for your sake. ³¹ Now is the judgment of this world; now shall the ruler of this world be cast out. ³² And I, if I be lifted up from the earth, will draw all men to Myself. ³³ But He said this signifying by what kind of death He was about to die. ³⁴ The crowd therefore answered Him, We have heard out of the law that

the Christ abides forever; and how *is it that* You say, The Son of Man must be lifted up? Who is this Son of Man? [35] Jesus then said to them, The light is still among you a little while. Walk while you have the light so that darkness may not overcome you; and he who walks in the darkness does not know where he is going. [36] While you have the light, believe into the light, so that you may become sons of light.

3. Religion's Unbelief and Blindness
vv. 36b-43

Jesus said these things, and He went away and was hidden from them. [37] But though He had done so many signs before them, they did not believe into Him, [38] That the word of the prophet Isaiah which he said might be fulfilled, "Lord, who has believed our report? And to whom has the arm of the Lord been revealed?" [39] For this *reason* they could not believe, because again Isaiah said, [40] "He has blinded their eyes and He hardened their heart, that they might not see with their eyes and understand with their heart and turn, and I will heal them." [41] These things said Isaiah because he saw His glory and spoke concerning Him. [42] Nevertheless even many of the rulers believed into Him, but because of the Pharisees they did not confess *Him,* so that they would not be put out of the synagogue; [43] For they loved the glory of men more than the glory of God.

4. Life's Declaration to the Unbelieving Religion
vv. 44-50

[44] But Jesus cried out and said, He who believes

into Me does not believe into Me, but into Him who sent Me; [45] And he who beholds Me beholds Him who sent Me. [46] I have come *as* a light into the world, that every one who believes into Me would not remain in darkness. [47] And if anyone hears My words and does not keep *them,* I do not judge him; for I have not come to judge the world, but to save the world. [48] He who rejects Me and does not receive My words has one who judges him; the word which I have spoken, that will judge him in the last day. [49] For I have not spoken from Myself; but the Father who sent Me, He Himself has given Me commandment, what to say and what to speak. [50] And I know that His commandment is eternal life. The things therefore that I speak, even as the Father has said to Me, so I speak.

CHAPTER 13

E. Life's Washing in Love to Maintain Fellowship
13:1-38

[1] Now before the Feast of the Passover, Jesus, knowing that His hour had come for Him to depart out of this world unto the Father, having loved His own who were in the world, He loved them to the uttermost. [2] And while supper was taking place, the devil having already put into the heart of Judas Iscariot, *the son* of Simon, that he should betray Him, [3] *Jesus,* knowing that the Father had given all into His hands and that He had come forth from God and was going to God, [4] Rose from supper and laid aside His outer garments; and taking a towel,

He girded Himself; [5] Then He poured water into the basin and began to wash the disciples' feet and to wipe *them* with the towel with which He was girded, [6] He came then to Simon Peter. *Peter* said to Him, Lord, do You wash my feet? [7] Jesus answered and said to him, What I am doing you do not know now, but you will know after these things. [8] Peter said to Him, You shall by no means wash my feet forever. Jesus answered him, Unless I wash you, you have no part with Me. [9] Simon Peter said to Him, Lord, not my feet only, but also my hands and my head. [10] Jesus said to him, He who is bathed has no need except to wash his feet, but is wholly clean; and you are clean, but not all *of you.* [11] For He knew the one betraying Him; for this reason He said, Not all of you are clean.

[12] Then when He had washed their feet and taken His outer garments and reclined *at the table* again, He said to them, Do you know what I have done to you? [13] You call Me the Teacher and the Lord, and you say rightly, for I am. [14] If I then, the Lord and the Teacher, have washed your feet, you also ought to wash one another's feet. [15] For I have given you an example so that you also may do even as I have done to you. [16] Truly, truly, I say to you, A slave is not greater than his master, nor one who is sent greater than the one who sends him. [17] If you know these things, blessed are you if you do them.

[18] I do not speak concerning all of you. I know whom I have chosen, but that the Scripture may be fulfilled, "He who eats bread with Me has lifted

up his heel against Me." [19] From now on I am telling you before it happens, so that when it happens, you may believe that I am. [20] Truly, truly, I say to you, He who receives whomever I shall send receives Me, and he who receives Me receives Him who sent Me.

[21] When Jesus had said these things, He became troubled in His spirit, and He testified and said, Truly, truly, I say to you that one of you will betray Me. [22] The disciples looked at one another, perplexed over whom He was speaking about. [23] One of His disciples, whom Jesus loved, was reclining on Jesus' bosom. [24] Simon Peter therefore nodded to him to inquire who it might be about whom He was speaking. [25] Then he, while reclining thus on Jesus' breast, said to Him, Lord, who is it? [26] Jesus answered, It is he for whom I will dip the morsel and to whom I will give *it*. And dipping the morsel, He gave *it* to Judas Iscariot, *the son* of Simon. [27] And at that moment, after the morsel, Satan entered into him. Jesus therefore said to him, What you do, do quickly. [28] But none of those reclining *at table* knew why He said this to him. [29] For some supposed, since Judas held the purse, that Jesus was saying to him, Buy the things that we have need of for the feast, or that he should give something to the poor. [30] Therefore having taken the morsel, he went out immediately; and it was night.

[31] Then when he went out, Jesus said, Now has the Son of Man been glorified, and God has been glorified in Him. [32] If God has been glorified in Him, God will also glorify Him in Himself, and He will

glorify Him immediately. [33] Little children, I am still with you a little while; you will seek Me, and even as I said to the Jews, Where I am going, you cannot come, now I say to you also. [34] A new commandment I give to you, that you love one another, even as I have loved you, that you also love one another. [35] By this shall all men know that you are My disciples, if you have love for one another.

[36] Simon Peter said to Him, Lord, where are You going? Jesus answered him, Where I go you cannot follow Me now, but you will follow later. [37] Peter said to Him, Lord, why can't I follow You now? I will lay down my life for You. [38] Jesus answered, Will you lay down your life for Me? Truly, truly, I say to you, A rooster shall by no means crow until you deny Me three times.

CHAPTER 14

II. Jesus Crucified and Christ Resurrected
Going to Prepare the Way to Bring Man into God,
and as the Spirit Coming to Abide and Live in the Believers
for the Building of God's Habitation
14:1—21:25

A. Life's Indwelling—For the Building of God's Habitation
14:1—16:33

1. The Dispensing of the Triune God—
For the Producing of His Abode
14:1-31

[1] Do not let your heart be troubled; believe into God, believe also into Me. [2] In My Father's house are many abodes; if *it were* not so, I would have told you; for I go to prepare a place for you. [3] And if I go

and prepare a place for you, I am coming again and will receive you to Myself, so that where I am you also may be. ⁴And where I am going you know the way. ⁵ Thomas said to Him, Lord, we do not know where You are going; how can we know the way? ⁶ Jesus said to him, I am the way and the reality and the life; no one comes to the Father except through Me.

⁷ If you had known Me, you would have known My Father also; and henceforth you know Him and have seen Him. ⁸ Philip said to Him, Lord, show us the Father and it is sufficient for us. ⁹ Jesus said to him, Have I been so long a time with you, and you have not known Me, Philip? He who has seen Me has seen the Father; how *is it that* you say, Show us the Father? ¹⁰ Do you not believe that I am in the Father and the Father is in Me? The words that I say to you I do not speak from Myself, but the Father who abides in Me does His works. ¹¹ Believe Me that I am in the Father and the Father is in Me; but if not, believe because of the works themselves. ¹² Truly, truly, I say to you, He who believes into Me, the works which I do he shall do also; and greater than these he shall do because I am going to the Father. ¹³And whatever you ask in My name, that I will do, that the Father may be glorified in the Son. ¹⁴ If you ask Me anything in My name, I will do *it*.

¹⁵ If you love Me, you will keep My commandments. ¹⁶And I will ask the Father, and He will give you another Comforter, that He may be with you forever, ¹⁷ *Even* the Spirit of reality, whom the world cannot receive, because it does not behold Him or

know *Him; but* you know Him, because He abides with you and shall be in you. [18] I will not leave you as orphans; I am coming to you. [19] Yet a little while and the world beholds Me no longer, but you behold Me; because I live, you also shall live. [20] In that day you will know that I *am* in My Father, and you in Me, and I in you.

[21] He who has My commandments and keeps them, he is the one who loves Me; and he who loves Me will be loved by My Father, and I will love him and will manifest Myself to him. [22] Judas, not Iscariot, said to Him, Lord, and what has happened that You are to manifest Yourself to us and not to the world? [23] Jesus answered and said to him, If anyone loves Me, he will keep My word, and My Father will love him, and We will come to him and make an abode with him. [24] He who does not love Me does not keep My words; and the word which you hear is not Mine, but the Father's who sent Me.

[25] These things I have spoken to you *while* abiding with you; [26] But the Comforter, the Holy Spirit, whom the Father will send in My name, He will teach you all things and remind you of all the things which I have said to you. [27] Peace I leave with you; My peace I give to you; not as the world gives do I give to you. Do not let your heart be troubled, neither let it be afraid. [28] You have heard that I said to you, I am going away and I am coming to you. If you loved Me, you would rejoice because I am going to the Father, for the Father is greater than I. [29] And now I have told you before it happens, so that when

it happens you may believe. [30] I will no longer speak much with you, for the ruler of the world is coming, and in Me he has nothing; [31] But *this is so* that the world may know that I love the Father, and as the Father commanded Me, so I do. Rise, let us go from here.

CHAPTER 15

2. The Organism of the Triune God in the Divine Dispensing 15:1—16:4

[1] I am the true vine, and My Father is the husbandman. [2] Every branch in Me that does not bear fruit, He takes it away; and every *branch* that bears fruit, He prunes it that it may bear more fruit. [3] You are already clean because of the word which I have spoken to you. [4] Abide in Me and I in you. As the branch cannot bear fruit of itself unless it abides in the vine, so neither *can* you unless you abide in Me. [5] I am the vine; you are the branches. He who abides in Me and I in him, he bears much fruit; for apart from Me you can do nothing. [6] If one does not abide in Me, he is cast out as a branch and is dried up; and they gather them and cast *them* into the fire, and they are burned. [7] If you abide in Me and My words abide in you, ask whatever you will, and it shall be done for you. [8] In this is My Father glorified, that you bear much fruit and so you will become My disciples. [9] As the Father has loved Me, I also have loved you; abide in My love. [10] If you keep My commandments, you will abide in My love; even as I have kept My Father's commandments

and abide in His love. [11] These things I have spoken to you that My joy may be in you and *that* your joy may be made full.

[12] This is My commandment, that you love one another even as I have loved you. [13] No one has greater love than this, that one lay down his life for his friends. [14] You are My friends if you do what I command you. [15] No longer do I call you slaves, for the slave does not know what his master is doing; but I have called you friends, for all the things which I have heard from My Father I have made known to you. [16] You did not choose Me, but I chose you, and I set you that you should go forth and bear fruit and *that* your fruit should remain, that whatever you ask the Father in My name, He may give you. [17] These things I command you that you may love one another.

[18] If the world hates you, know that it has hated Me before you. [19] If you were of the world, the world would love its own; but because you are not of the world, but I chose you out of the world, therefore the world hates you. [20] Remember the word which I said to you, A slave is not greater than his master. If they have persecuted Me, they will persecute you also; if they have kept My word, they will keep yours also. [21] But all these things they will do to you because of My name, because they do not know Him who sent Me. [22] If I had not come and spoken to them, they would not have sin; but now they have no excuse for their sin. [23] He who hates Me hates My Father also. [24] If I did not do among them the works which no one else has done, they would not have

sin; but now they have both seen and hated both Me and My Father. [25] But *it is so* that the word written in their law may be fulfilled, "They hated Me without cause." [26] But when the Comforter comes, whom I will send to you from the Father, the Spirit of reality, who proceeds from the Father, He will testify concerning Me; [27] And you testify also, because from the beginning you have been with Me.

CHAPTER 16

[1] These things I have spoken to you so that you would not be stumbled. [2] They will put you out of the synagogues; but an hour is coming for every one who kills you to think that he is offering service to God. [3] And these things they will do because they have not known the Father nor Me. [4] But these things I have spoken to you that when their hour comes you may remember them, that I told you *of them*. Now these things I have not said to you from the beginning, because I was with you.

3. The Work of the Spirit Consummating in the Mingling of Divinity with Humanity
16:5-33

[5] But now I am going to Him who sent Me; and none of you asks Me, Where are You going? [6] But because I have spoken these things to you, sorrow has filled your heart. [7] But I tell you the truth, It is expedient for you that I go away; for if I do not go away, the Comforter will not come to you; but if I go, I will send Him to you.

[8] And when He comes, He will convict the world

concerning sin and concerning righteousness and concerning judgment: [9] Concerning sin, because they do not believe into Me; [10] And concerning righteousness, because I am going to the Father and you no longer behold Me; [11] And concerning judgment, because the ruler of this world has been judged.

[12] I have yet many things to say to you, but you cannot bear *them* now. [13] But when He, the Spirit of reality, comes, He will guide you into all the reality; for He will not speak from Himself, but what He hears He will speak; and He will declare to you the things that are coming. [14] He will glorify Me, for He will receive of Mine and will declare *it* to you. [15] All that the Father has is Mine; for this *reason* I have said that He receives of Mine and will declare *it* to you.

[16] A little while and you no longer behold Me, and again a little while and you will see Me. [17] *Some* of His disciples then said to one another, What is this that He says to us, A little while and you do not behold Me, and again a little while and you will see Me; and, Because I am going to the Father? [18] Therefore they said, What is this that He says, A little while? We do not know what He is talking about. [19] Jesus knew that they wanted to ask Him and He said to them, Are you inquiring among yourselves concerning this, that I said, A little while and you do not behold Me, and again a little while and you will see Me? [20] Truly, truly, I say to you that you will weep and lament, but the world will rejoice; you will be sorrowful, but your sorrow will be turned into joy. [21] A woman, when she

gives birth, has sorrow because her hour has come; but when she brings forth the little child, she no longer remembers the affliction because of the joy that a man has been born into the world. [22] Therefore you also now have sorrow; but I will see you again and your heart will rejoice, and no one takes your joy away from you. [23] And in that day you will ask Me nothing. Truly, truly, I say to you, Whatever you ask the Father in My name, He will give to you. [24] Until now you have asked for nothing in My name; ask and you shall receive, that your joy may be made full.

[25] These things I have spoken to you in parables; an hour is coming when I will no longer speak to you in parables, but I will report to you plainly concerning the Father. [26] In that day you will ask in My name, and I do not say to you that I will ask the Father concerning you, [27] For the Father Himself loves you, because you have loved Me and have believed that I came forth from God. [28] I came forth out from the Father and have come into the world; again, I am leaving the world and am going to the Father. [29] His disciples said, Behold, now You are speaking plainly and not saying any parable. [30] Now we know that You know all things and have no need that anyone ask You; by this we believe that You came forth from God. [31] Jesus answered them, Do you now believe? [32] Behold, an hour is coming, and has come, that you will be scattered each to his own place and will leave Me alone; yet I am not alone, because the Father is with Me. [33] These things I have spoken to you that in Me you may have peace. In the world you

have affliction, but take courage; I have overcome
the world.

CHAPTER 17

B. Life's Prayer
17:1-26

1. The Son to Be Glorified
That the Father May Be Glorified
vv. 1-5

[1] These things Jesus spoke, and lifting up His
eyes to heaven, He said, Father, the hour has come;
glorify Your Son that the Son may glorify You;
[2] Even as You have given Him authority over all
flesh to give eternal life to all whom You have given
Him. [3] And this is eternal life, that they may know
You, the only true God, and Him whom You have
sent, Jesus Christ. [4] I have glorified You on earth,
finishing the work which You have given Me to do.
[5] And now, glorify Me along with Yourself, Father,
with the glory which I had with You before the
world was.

2. The Believers to Be Built Up into One
vv. 6-24

[6] I have manifested Your name to the men whom
You gave Me out of the world. They were Yours, and
You gave them to Me, and they have kept Your word.
[7] Now they have come to know that all that You have
given Me is from You, [8] For the words which You
gave Me I have given to them, and they received
them and knew truly that I came forth from You, and

they have believed that You sent Me. [9] I ask concerning them; I do not ask concerning the world, but concerning *those* whom You have given Me, for they are Yours; [10] And all that is Mine is Yours, and Yours Mine; and I have been glorified in them. [11] And I am no longer in the world; yet they are in the world, and I am coming to You. Holy Father, keep them in Your name, which You have given to Me, that they may be one even as We are. [12] When I was with them, I kept them in Your name, which You have given to Me, and I guarded *them;* and not one of them perished, except the son of perdition, that the Scripture might be fulfilled. [13] But now I am coming to You, and these things I speak in the world that they may have My joy made full in themselves.

[14] I have given them Your word, and the world has hated them, because they are not of the world even as I am not of the world. [15] I do not ask that You would take them out of the world, but that You would keep them out of *the hands of* the evil *one.* [16] They are not of the world, even as I am not of the world. [17] Sanctify them in the truth; Your word is truth. [18] As you have sent Me into the world, I also have sent them into the world. [19] And for their sake I sanctify Myself, that they themselves also may be sanctified in truth. [20] And I do not ask concerning these only, but concerning those also who believe into Me through their word, [21] That they all may be one; even as You, Father, are in Me and I in You, that they also may be in Us; that the world may believe that You have sent Me.

[22] And the glory which You have given Me I have

given to them, that they may be one, even as We are one; [23] I in them, and You in Me, that they may be perfected into one, that the world may know that You have sent Me and have loved them even as You have loved Me. [24] Father, *concerning* that which You have given Me, I desire that they also may be with Me where I am, that they may behold My glory, which You have given Me, for You loved Me before the foundation of the world.

3. The Father to Be Shown Righteous in Loving the Son and His Believers
vv. 25-26

[25] Righteous Father, though the world has not known You, yet I have known You, and these have known that You have sent Me. [26] And I have made Your name known to them and will *yet* make *it* known, that the love with which You have loved Me may be in them, and I in them.

CHAPTER 18

C. Life's Process through Death and Resurrection for Multiplication
18:1—20:13, 17

1. Delivering Himself in Voluntary Boldness to Be Processed
18:1-11

[1] When Jesus had said these things, He went forth with His disciples across the brook Kedron, where there was a garden, into which He entered as well as His disciples. [2] And Judas also, who was betraying Him, knew the place, for Jesus often

gathered there with His disciples. [3] Then Judas, having gotten the cohort and some attendants from the chief priests and Pharisees, came there with torches and lamps and weapons. [4] Jesus therefore, knowing all the things that were coming upon Him, went forth and said to them, Whom do you seek? [5] They answered Him, Jesus the Nazarene. He said to them, I am. And Judas also, who was betraying Him, was standing with them. [6] When therefore He said to them, I am, they drew back and fell to the ground. [7] Then again He asked them, Whom do you seek? And they said, Jesus the Nazarene. [8] Jesus answered, I told you that I am; if therefore you seek Me, let these go away, [9] That the word might be fulfilled which He spoke, Of those whom You have given Me, I have not lost one. [10] Then Simon Peter, having a sword, drew it and struck the slave of the high priest and cut off his right ear; and the slave's name was Malchus. [11] Jesus therefore said to Peter, Put the sword into its sheath. The cup which the Father has given Me, shall I not drink it?

2. Examined in His Dignity by Mankind
18:12-38a

[12] Then the cohort and the commander and the attendants of the Jews seized Jesus and bound Him [13] And led *Him* away to Annas first; for he was the father-in-law of Caiaphas, who was high priest that year. [14] Now it was Caiaphas who had advised the Jews that it was expedient for one man to die for the people. [15] And Simon Peter followed Jesus, as well as another disciple. And that disciple was

known to the high priest, and he entered with Jesus into the court of the high priest; [16] But Peter stood at the door outside. Then the other disciple, the one known to the high priest, went out and spoke to *the maid* who kept the door and brought Peter in. [17] Then the maid who kept the door said to Peter, Are you not also *one* of this man's disciples? He said, I am not. [18] Now the slaves and the attendants were standing *there,* having made a fire of coals, for it was cold, and they were warming themselves; and Peter also was with them, standing and warming himself. [19] The high priest then questioned Jesus concerning His disciples and concerning His teaching. [20] Jesus answered him, I have spoken openly to the world; I always taught in the synagogue and in the temple, where all the Jews come together, and I spoke nothing in secret. [21] Why do you question Me? Question those who have heard *Me, concerning* what I spoke to them; behold, these know what I said. [22] And when He said these things, one of the attendants standing by slapped Jesus, saying, Is that how You answer the high priest? [23] Jesus answered him, If I have spoken wrongly, testify concerning the wrong; but if rightly, why do you strike Me? [24] Annas then sent Him bound to Caiaphas the high priest.

[25] Now Simon Peter was standing and warming himself. Then they said to him, Are you not also *one* of His disciples? He denied and said, I am not. [26] One of the slaves of the high priest, who was a relative of him whose ear Peter had cut off, said, Did I not see you in the garden with

Him? [27] Then Peter denied again, and immediately a rooster crowed.

[28] Then they led Jesus from Caiaphas into the praetorium, and it was early morning. And they themselves did not enter into the praetorium, so that they would not be defiled, but might eat the passover. [29] Pilate therefore went outside to them and said, What accusation do you bring against this man? [30] They answered and said to him, If this man were not doing evil, we would not have delivered Him to you. [31] Pilate said then to them, You take Him and judge Him according to your law. The Jews said to him, It is not lawful for us to kill anyone, [32] That the word of Jesus might be fulfilled which He spoke, signifying by what kind of death He was to die. [33] Pilate therefore entered again into the praetorium and called for Jesus. And he said to Him, You are the King of the Jews?

[34] Jesus answered, Are you saying this of yourself, or did others tell you about Me? [35] Pilate answered, Am I a Jew? Your nation and its chief priests have delivered You to me. What have You done? [36] Jesus answered, My kingdom is not of this world. If My kingdom were of this world, My attendants would be struggling so that I would not be delivered to the Jews; but as it is, My kingdom is not from here. [37] Pilate said therefore to Him, So then You are a king? Jesus answered, You say that I am a king. For this I have been born, and for this I have come into the world, that I would testify to the truth. Every one who is of the truth hears My voice. [38] Pilate said to Him, What is truth?

3. Sentenced in Man's Injustice
by Blind Religion with Dark Politics
18:38b—19:16

And having said this, he again went out to the
Jews and said to them, I find no fault in Him. [39] But
you have a custom that I release one man to you at
the Passover. Is it your will therefore that I release
to you the King of the Jews? [40] Then they cried out
again, saying, Not this man, but Barabbas. Now
Barabbas was a robber.

CHAPTER 19

[1] Therefore at that time Pilate took Jesus and
scourged *Him.* [2] And the soldiers wove a crown of
thorns and put it on His head, and they threw a purple garment around Him. [3] And they came to Him
and said, Rejoice, King of the Jews! and slapped
Him. [4] And Pilate went outside again and said to
them, Behold, I am bringing Him out to you that you
may know that I find no fault in Him. [5] Then Jesus
came out, wearing the thorny crown and the purple
garment. And he said to them, Behold, the man!
[6] When therefore the chief priests and the attendants saw Him, they cried out, saying, Crucify!
Crucify! Pilate said to them, You take Him and crucify *Him,* for I do not find fault in Him. [7] The Jews
answered him, We have a law, and according to that
law He ought to die because He made Himself
the Son of God. [8] When Pilate therefore heard this
word, he became frightened the more, [9] And he entered into the praetorium again and said to Jesus,
Where are You from? But Jesus gave him no answer.

[10] Therefore Pilate said to Him, You do not speak to me? Do You not know that I have authority to release You and I have authority to crucify You? [11] Jesus answered him, You would have no authority against Me if it were not given to you from above; for this *reason,* he who has delivered Me to you has the greater sin. [12] From then on, Pilate sought to release Him, but the Jews cried out, saying, If you release this man, you are not a friend of Caesar; every one who makes himself a king opposes Caesar. [13] Pilate therefore, when he heard these words, brought Jesus outside and sat down on the judgment seat in a place called the Pavement, but in Hebrew, Gabbatha. [14] Now it was the *day of* preparation for the Passover; it was about the sixth hour. And he said to the Jews, Behold, your King! [15] They cried out then, Take *Him* away! Take *Him* away! Crucify Him! Pilate said to them, Shall I crucify your King? The chief priests answered, We have no king except Caesar. [16] Therefore at that time he delivered Him to them that He might be crucified. Therefore they took Jesus.

4. Tested in God's Sovereignty by Death
19:17-30

[17] And bearing the cross for Himself, He went out to the *place* called the Place of a Skull, which is called in Hebrew, Golgotha, [18] Where they crucified Him, and with Him two others, on this side and that, and Jesus in the middle. [19] And Pilate wrote a notice also and put *it* on the cross; and it was written, JESUS THE NAZARENE, THE KING

OF THE JEWS. [20] This notice therefore many of the Jews read, for the place where Jesus was crucified was near the city, and it was written in Hebrew, in Latin, *and* in Greek. [21] The chief priests of the Jews therefore said to Pilate, Do not write, The King of the Jews, but that He said, I am the King of the Jews. [22] Pilate answered, What I have written, I have written.

[23] The soldiers then, when they had crucified Jesus, took His garments and made four parts, a part for each soldier, *and they took* the tunic as well. But the tunic was seamless, woven from the top throughout. [24] They said therefore to one another, Let us not tear it, but let us cast lots for it *to see* whose it shall be, that the Scripture might be fulfilled which says, "They divided My garments among themselves, and for My clothing they cast lots." So then the soldiers did these things. [25] And there were standing by the cross of Jesus His mother and His mother's sister *and* Mary the *wife* of Clopas and Mary the Magdalene. [26] Then Jesus, seeing His mother and the disciple whom He loved standing by, said to His mother, Woman, behold, your son. [27] Then He said to the disciple, Behold, your mother. And from that hour the disciple took her into his own *home.*

[28] After this, Jesus, knowing that all things had now been finished *and* so that the Scripture might be fulfilled, said, I thirst. [29] There was lying *there* a vessel full of vinegar; therefore, they put a spongefull of vinegar on hyssop and brought it to His mouth. [30] Then when Jesus had taken the vinegar,

He said, It is finished! And He bowed His head and delivered up His spirit.

5. Issuing in Blood and Water
19:31-37

[31] Then the Jews, since it was the *day of* preparation *and* so that the bodies might not remain on the cross on the Sabbath (for that Sabbath day was a great *Sabbath*), requested of Pilate that their legs might be broken and that they might be taken away. [32] The soldiers therefore came and broke the legs of the first man and of the other man who had been crucified with Him. [33] But coming to Jesus, when they saw that He had already died, they did not break His legs; [34] But one of the soldiers pierced His side with a spear, and immediately there came out blood and water. [35] And he who has seen *this* has testified, and his testimony is true; and he knows that he says what is true, that you also may believe. [36] For these things happened that the Scripture might be fulfilled: "No bone of His shall be broken." [37] And again another Scripture says, "They shall look on Him whom they pierced."

6. Resting in Human Honor
19:38-42

[38] And after these things Joseph from Arimathea, being a disciple of Jesus, but a hidden one for fear of the Jews, requested of Pilate that he might take the body of Jesus away; and Pilate allowed *it*. He came therefore and took His body away. [39] And Nicodemus, he who had come to Him

the first time by night, came also, bringing a mix-
ture of myrrh and aloes of about a hundred pounds.
[40] Therefore they took the body of Jesus and bound
it in linen cloths with the spices, as is the custom of
the Jews for burying. [41] Now in the place where He
was crucified there was a garden, and in the garden
a new tomb, in which no one had ever yet been laid.
[42] Therefore because of the *day of* preparation for
the Jews *and* because the tomb was near, they laid
Jesus there.

CHAPTER 20

7. Resurrecting in Divine Glory
20:1-13, 17

[1] Now on the first day of the week, Mary the
Magdalene came early to the tomb while it was yet
dark and saw the stone taken away from the tomb.
[2] She ran therefore and came to Simon Peter and
to the other disciple whom Jesus loved and said to
them, They have taken away the Lord out of the
tomb, and we do not know where they have laid
Him. [3] Peter therefore went forth, as well as the
other disciple, and came to the tomb. [4] And the two
ran together, yet the other disciple ran ahead faster
than Peter and came first to the tomb. [5] And stoop-
ing to look in, he saw the linen cloths lying *there;*
however, he did not enter. [6] Then Simon Peter also
came, following him, and entered into the tomb;
and he beheld the linen cloths lying *there* [7] And the
handkerchief which had been over His head, not lying with the linen cloths, but folded up in one place
apart. [8] At that time therefore the other disciple

also, who came first to the tomb, entered, and he saw and believed; [9] For as yet they did not understand the Scripture, that He had to rise from among the dead. [10] The disciples therefore went away again to their own *home.*

[11] But Mary stood outside at the tomb weeping. Then as she wept, she stooped to look into the tomb [12] And beheld two angels in white sitting, one at the head and one at the feet, where the body of Jesus had lain. [13] And they said to her, Woman, why are you weeping? She said to them, Because they have taken away my Lord, and I do not know where they have laid Him.

D. Life in Resurrection
20:14—21:25

1. Appearing to the Seekers
and Ascending to the Father
20:14-18

[14] When she said these things, she turned backward and beheld Jesus standing *there,* yet she did not know that it was Jesus. [15] Jesus said to her, Woman, why are you weeping? Whom are you seeking? She, supposing that He was the gardener, said to Him, Sir, if you have carried Him away, tell me where you have laid Him, and I will take Him away. [16] Jesus said to her, Mary! She turned and said to Him in Hebrew, Rabboni! (which means Teacher). [17] Jesus said to her. Do not touch Me, for I have not yet ascended to the Father; but go to My brothers and say to them, I ascend to My Father and your Father, and My God and your God. [18] Mary the

Magdalene came, announcing to the disciples, I have seen the Lord, and *that* He had said these things to her.

2. Coming as the Spirit to Be Breathed into the Believers
20:19-25

[19] When therefore it was evening on that day, the first day of the week, and while the doors were shut where the disciples were for fear of the Jews, Jesus came and stood in the midst and said to them, Peace be to you. [20] And when He had said this, He showed them His hands and His side. The disciples therefore rejoiced at seeing the Lord. [21] Then Jesus said to them again, Peace be to you; as the Father has sent Me, I also send you. [22] And when He had said this, He breathed into *them* and said to them, Receive the Holy Spirit. [23] Whosever sins you forgive, they are forgiven them; and whosever *sins* you retain, they are retained.

[24] But Thomas, one of the twelve, called Didymus, was not with them when Jesus came. [25] The other disciples therefore said to him, We have seen the Lord! But he said to them, Unless I see in His hands the mark of the nails and put my finger into the mark of the nails and put my hand into His side, I will by no means believe.

3. Meeting with the Believers
20:26-31

[26] And after eight days, His disciples were again within, and Thomas *was* with them. Jesus came, though the doors were shut, and stood in the midst

and said, Peace be to you. [27] Then He said to Thomas, Bring your finger here and see My hands, and bring your hand and put *it* into My side; and do not be unbelieving, but believing. [28] Thomas answered and said to Him, My Lord and my God! [29] Jesus said to him, Because you have seen Me, you have believed. Blessed are those who have not seen and have believed. [30] Moreover indeed many other signs also Jesus did before His disciples, which are not written in this book. [31] But these have been written that you may believe that Jesus is the Christ, the Son of God, and that believing, you may have life in His name.

CHAPTER 21

4. Moving and Living with the Believers
21:1-14

[1] After these things Jesus manifested Himself again to the disciples at the Sea of Tiberias. And He manifested *Himself* in this way: [2] Simon Peter and Thomas, called Didymus, and Nathanael from Cana of Galilee and the *sons* of Zebedee and two others of His disciples were *there* together. [3] Simon Peter said to them, I am going fishing. They said to him, We also are coming with you. They went forth and got into the boat, and that night they caught nothing. [4] Now as soon as the morning broke, Jesus stood on the shore; however the disciples did not know that it was Jesus. [5] Then Jesus said to them, Little children, you do not have any *fish* to eat, do you? They answered Him, No. [6] And He said to them, Cast the

net on the right side of the boat, and you will find
some. They cast therefore, and they were no longer
able to haul it *in* because of the abundance of fish.
[7] Then that disciple whom Jesus loved said to Peter,
It is the Lord! Therefore when Simon Peter heard
that it was the Lord, he put his outer garment
around himself, for he was naked; and he threw
himself into the sea. [8] But the other disciples came
in the little boat, for they were not far from the land,
but about two hundred cubits away, dragging the
net of fish. [9] Then when they got out onto the land,
they saw a fire of coals laid *there,* and fish lying on
it and bread. [10] Jesus said to them, Bring *some* of
the fish that you have just now caught. [11] Simon Peter therefore went up and hauled the net to the land
full of large fish, a hundred and fifty-three; and
though there were so many, the net was not torn.
[12] Jesus said to them, Come *and* have breakfast.
But none of the disciples dared to inquire of Him,
Who are you? knowing that it was the Lord. [13] Jesus
came and took the bread and gave *it* to them, and
the fish likewise. [14] This was now the third time that
Jesus was manifested to the disciples after He had
been raised from the dead.

5. Working and Walking with the Believers
21:15-25

[15] Then when they had eaten breakfast, Jesus
said to Simon Peter, Simon, *son* of John, do you love
Me more than these? He said to Him, Yes, Lord, You
know that I love You. He said to him, Feed My
lambs. [16] He said to him again a second time, Simon,

son of John, do you love Me? He said to Him, Yes, Lord, You know that I love You. He said to him, Shepherd My sheep. [17] He said to him the third time, Simon, *son* of John, do you love Me? Peter was grieved that He said to him the third time, Do you love Me? And he said to Him, Lord, You know all things; You know that I love You. Jesus said to him, Feed My sheep. [18] Truly, truly, I say to you, When you were younger, you girded yourself and walked where you wished; but when you grow old, you will stretch out your hands, and another will gird you and carry *you* where you do not wish *to go*. [19] Now this He said, signifying by what kind of death he would glorify God. And when He had said this, He said to him, Follow Me. [20] Peter, turning around, saw the disciple whom Jesus loved following, who also reclined on His breast at the supper, and said, Lord, who is the one betraying You? [21] Peter therefore, seeing him, said to Jesus, Lord, and what about this man? [22] Jesus said to him, If I want him to remain until I come, what *is that* to you? You follow Me. [23] This word therefore went out among the brothers, that that disciple would not die, yet Jesus did not say to him that he would not die, but, If I want him to remain until I come, what is *that* to you?

[24] This is the disciple who testifies concerning these things, and the one who has written these things; and we know that his testimony is true. [25] And there are also many other things which Jesus did, which, if they were written one by one, I suppose that not even the world itself could contain the books written.

The First Step
in Living a Christian Life

Perhaps you have wondered what kind of life God wants you to live. You may already know that the Bible is a wonderful book, but perhaps you do not know what it says about the kind of life a Christian ought to live. The following article, based on the Gospel of John, explains how you can live the life God desires you to live. It tells you who you are and what you can do to experience the divine things of God's salvation. Please read it carefully and prayerfully.

The Gospel of John reveals that in Christ, the Word of God, is life (1:4); that He came that man may have life (10:10b); and that He Himself is life (11:25; 14:6). Furthermore, this Gospel shows us that Christ is the bread of life (6:35); that He has the water of life (4:14); that He gives life to man (5:21); and that He even lives in man as life (14:19). [1]

Man was made as a vessel to contain God as life. However, by creation he was merely an empty vessel; he did not have genuine life. The created life of man is not genuine; genuine life is the divine life, which is in Christ. The life we have before we receive Christ is, at best, a temporary life; it is not a permanent life, an everlasting life. Although it is an instant life, it is not a constant one. Before we receive Christ we are uncertain just how long our instant life will endure. Thus, in a sense, before we are saved we do not have life. The life in Christ is eternal, constant, and permanent. All men need such a life, the divine and uncreated life that is in Christ. This life is for man, and man is the receiver of this life. [2]

Chapter three through chapter eleven of the Gospel of John relate nine cases to expose the condition and need of man, and then they reveal how the Lord can deal with all the conditions and meet all the needs of man. Only God's life can meet the need of man's every case. We must realize that life here means the Lord Himself (1:4), the Word which was God (1:1) and which became flesh (1:14). Although the Lord might have dealt with thousands of human cases, the Gospel of John selected only nine of them to illustrate how the Lord as life could and still can meet the need of every human case.

MAN'S CONDITION AND NEED

Let us see, first of all, the condition of man in each case. The first case, in chapter three, is about a high-class, moral person who came to the Lord (3:1-13). He is a superior gentleman, highly cultured, very religious, God-seeking, and God-fearing. The second case, in chapter four, shows forth exactly the opposite condition (4:1-42). The first case is about a moral man; the second case is about an immoral woman. The former is about a mild, high-class person, while the latter is about a wild, low-class person. This wicked woman had had five husbands and was living with a sixth who was not her husband. The third case, also in chapter four, is about a young man who was sick and about to die (4:46-54). The fourth case, in chapter five, is about a man who had been sick for thirty-eight years (5:1-4). He was utterly weak and unable to move even one step. The fifth case, in chapter six, is about the hungry multitude who were seeking something to feed on (6:1-15). The sixth case, in chapter seven, is about the thirsty people whose thirst could not be quenched by the best religion or by anything of this life (7:37-39). The seventh case, in chapter eight, sets forth a sinful woman who committed a terrible sin and who was under the condemnation and bondage of her sin (8:2-11). The eighth case, in chapters nine and ten, concerns a blind man who was born blind (9:1-38). Finally, the ninth case, in chapter eleven, is about Lazarus, who died and was buried for four days (11:1-44).

The conditions of the people mentioned in these nine cases represent the conditions of all men. Some men are good like Nicodemus, while others are wicked like the Samaritan woman. Others, like the young man in Capernaum, are dying. Most are weak like the man who was sick for thirty-eight years. They desire to do good, but they do not have the strength to fulfill that desire. They know religion, but, because they are weak, they do not have the power to live out its standards or fulfill its regulations. Other people are hungry, craving for something to enjoy, while some are thirsting for something more than their human life can offer them. There are some people whose thirst is so great that nothing in this life can satisfy them. Some people continually commit sins and are under the condemnation and bondage of their sins. Some, like the blind man, are blind, not physically, but psychologically and spiritually. Finally, the last condition of all men is death, for they are in death and, at the same time, are on the road to death. They are dead already and yet they all will die later. All men are dead men who are going to die. Therefore, these nine cases portray the true conditions of all men. These conditions speak forth man's need, which only the Lord as life can fully meet.

EACH INDIVIDUAL'S CONDITION AND NEED

All the conditions of these nine cases can also be found in each individual person. One person can possess all the conditions of all men. For example, you may be a good man, or, at least you have the intention of being a good man. You may also be quite religious, fearing God and seeking Him. At the same time, however, you may also have done something mean, something which is not honorable. You may be a religious gentleman with high morals and yet have done something low. On the one hand, you are a high-class person; on the other hand, you are a low-class person.

You are also sick and about to die morally and spiritually. You may be very living physically, but you are dying morally and spiritually. Even physically you are also dying day by day. Apparently you are living; actually you are dying.

Another condition of yours is that you are a weak person. You know that you should do good and you know what is right, but you lack the strength or the power to do it. Perhaps you are not yet twenty-five years old, but you have been sick for "thirty-eight years" (5:5). You know that you should love others, but you are weak; you want to keep all the laws of God and you desire to please God, but you are unable to do so. In other words, you have the desire to do good, but you do not have the ability to perform what you desire. You need the proper power of life.

Hunger and thirst are also two items of your condition. Many times you feel that you are a hungry person; many times you are thirsty for education, for money, or for pleasure. You need the Lord as the bread of life to satisfy your hunger, and you need the Lord's living water to quench your thirst.

Another condition that can also be found in you as an individual is your sinfulness. You are sinful. You are a sinner and you commit sin. You need the forgiveness of the Lord as well as deliverance from the bondage of sin.

In another respect, you are in a state of blindness. Even though you may have perfect vision with your physical eyes, you cannot perceive the meaning of human life, and especially you cannot see spiritual things. You are blind and you need the Lord to open your eyes and to give you sight.

Your last condition is that of a dead man who eventually will die. Have you ever realized that you are a dead person? No one is alive in spirit—everyone is dead. You need the resurrection life of the Lord Jesus.

Every person has, in his fallen condition, every aspect of these nine cases. Every person, to a certain degree at least, is in each of these conditions. Every condition is an indication of everyone's real need.

THE LORD'S SUFFICIENCY
IN MEETING MAN'S NEED

We have seen the condition and need of man in these nine cases. Now we must see how the Lord is able to come into man's fallen condition and meet his every need. In every case, the Lord presents Himself as the One who can fulfill the deficiencies of man. These nine cases fully prove the Lord's sufficiency to meet man's every need.

The first case shows that the Lord can afford us regeneration (3:3, 5), which even a superior person such as Nicodemus needed that he might have the life of God for the entrance into the kingdom of God. The case of the Samaritan woman, a sinful and unsatisfied woman, reveals how much the Lord can satisfy such a person with His living water (4:10). For the case of the dying man, the Lord is the healing power of life (4:50). The case of the weak man who had been sick for thirty-eight years demonstrates the enlivening power of the Lord's life (5:8-9). In the case of the hungry multitude which needed something to feed on, the Lord presents Himself as the bread of life (6:47, 48). In the case of the thirsty people, the Lord assures them that He can quench their thirst by the flowing river of living water (7:37, 38). In the case of the woman living in sin, we see that the Lord is able to deliver such a one from her sinful situation and release her from the bondage of sin (8:34-36). In the case of the blind man, the Lord opens his eyes and gives him sight (9:5-7). Finally, in the case of Lazarus, who had died, had been buried, and was even decaying in the grave, the power of the Lord's resurrection life is fully exhibited (11:25).

In all of these cases the Lord's sufficiency in meeting man's need is adequately proved. There is not one of man's conditions that He cannot solve. There is not a need that He cannot meet. He is able! He is sufficient! He can deal with all our problems and supply all our needs! Praise His name!

REGENERATION—THE PREREQUISITE
TO FULL SALVATION

All aspects of the Lord's work as shown and signified in these nine cases are the different aspects of the Lord's full salvation, which are 1) regeneration, 2) the satisfaction with the living water, 3) the healing power of life, 4) the enlivening with the power of life, 5) the feeding with the bread of life, 6) the quenching of thirst with the rivers of living water, 7) the deliverance from sin, 8) the opening of the blind eyes, and 9) resurrection. All of these items are included in the Lord's salvation.

The first of these items is regeneration. Regeneration is the start of the spiritual life. All spiritual experiences begin with regeneration. If we have regeneration, we are then qualified to participate in all the other items of the Lord's salvation. Regeneration is a prerequisite to the experience of all the other items of the Lord's salvation. This is the reason that the case of regeneration is recorded as the first one. All the experiences of the other items depend upon the experience of regeneration. Before we can be satisfied with the living water, we must first be regenerated. The living water issues from the initial experience of regeneration. Without regeneration, the Lord's living water can never be in you. The principle is the same with all the other experiences. A dying person needs to be regenerated that he may be healed and live eternally. A weak person must first be regenerated; then he can be enlivened with the power of life. A person must first be regenerated before he can feed upon the Lord as the bread of life. To enjoy the nourishment of life depends very much upon regeneration. To have the flow of living water is also dependent upon regeneration. If you are not regenerated, you could never have your thirst quenched by the Lord's living water. To be delivered from sin and to have our blind eyes opened both require that we first be regenerated. Without regeneration, it is impossible for anyone to partake of the deliverance from sin or to receive spiritual sight. Furthermore, no one can participate in resurrection life before experiencing regeneration. The Lord's salvation begins with regeneration and ends with resurrection life. Thus, we need to examine very carefully the first case, the case of Nicodemus, which reveals man's need for regeneration.

REGENERATION

The first case, that of Nicodemus, is the case of regeneration. Nicodemus was a person of the highest class, and we need to consider his virtues and attributes. First, he was a teacher with the highest attainment in education. As a teacher of the Jews, he taught the Old Testament, the Sacred Word. Second, Nicodemus was "a ruler of the Jews." He had a position with a certain amount of honor and authority. Third, he was an old man. As an old man, he had a good deal of experience. He was a man full of experiences. Fourth, he was undoubtedly a moral man, a good man. If you look at the way he talked, you will realize that he was a moral man. Fifth, Nicodemus was a man who was truly seeking after God. Although he was somewhat fearful of the Pharisees, he still came to the Lord Jesus by night. This indicated that he was seeking God. Sixth, he was very humble. Nicodemus was an old man of perhaps sixty or seventy years of age, yet he came to see the Lord Jesus, who was only a little over thirty years of age. That such an experienced, educated, and elderly man would come to see someone much younger than he indicates his humility. Furthermore, although Nicodemus was a teacher, he addressed the Lord Jesus as Rabbi. Among the Jews, to call a person Rabbi means that you are humbling yourself. Seventh, Nicodemus was an honest man. His speech reveals his honesty. Can you find a better person than Nicodemus? He was a man of a superior standard, high attainment, and morality.

When Nicodemus came to the Lord Jesus, the Lord took the opportunity to reveal the true need of mankind. In His conversation with Nicodemus, the Lord revealed that regardless of how good we are, we still need regeneration. Regeneration is the first need of man. Moral people, as well as immoral people, need regeneration. Many Christians hold the mistaken concept that people need regeneration simply because they are fallen. However, if man had never fallen, he still would have needed regeneration. Even if Adam had not fallen, he still would have needed regeneration. That was why God put him in front of the tree of life. If Adam had partaken of the tree of life, he would have been regenerated.

Since we are human beings, we all have a human life. The problem is not a matter of whether or not our human life is good or bad. Regardless of the kind of human life we have, as long as we do not have the divine life, we need to be regenerated. To be regenerated simply means to have the divine life besides our human life. God's eternal purpose is that man be a vessel to contain the divine life. Our being with our human life is a vessel to contain God as life. The divine life is God's goal. The divine life is God Himself. God's goal is that we, as people with a human life, receive the divine life into our being as our real life. This is the true meaning of regeneration. Many Christians are not clear about this fact, thinking that regeneration is necessary simply because we are fallen and sinful. According to this concept, we need to be regenerated because our life is bad and cannot be improved. This concept is wrong. I say once again that even if Adam in the garden of Eden had never fallen, he still would have needed to be regenerated, to be born again, that he might have another life, the life of God. Therefore, to be regenerated is to receive the divine life, God Himself.

What is the meaning of regeneration? Regeneration is not any kind of outward improvement or cultivation; neither is it only a mere change or con version without life. Regeneration is a rebirth which brings in a new life. It is absolutely a matter of life, not a matter of doing. Regeneration is simply to have a life other than the life we already have. We have already received the human life from our parents; now we need to receive the divine life from God. Hence, regeneration means to have the divine life of God in addition to the human life which we already possess. Therefore, regeneration requires another birth in order to possess another life. To be regenerated, to be born again, does not mean to adjust or correct ourselves. It means to have the life of God, just as to be born of our parents means to have the life of our parents. To be regenerated is to be born of God (John 1:13), and to be born of God is to have the life of God, that is, the eternal life (3:15-16). If we have the life of God, we are the sons of God. The life of God gives us the right to become the sons of God (John 1:12), because by this life we have the divine nature of God (2 Pet. 1:4) and have the life-relationship with God, that is, the sonship (Rom. 8:15; Gal. 4:56).

A. Man's and Religion's False Concept— the Need of Better Teaching to Improve Man

Due to human culture and the Jewish religion, Nicodemus thought that man needed to behave.

Since man must have good conduct and worship God in a proper way, man needs much teaching. Nicodemus considered Christ to be a teacher come from God. This indicates that he might have thought that he needed better teachings to improve himself. But the Lord's answer in the following verse unveiled to him that his need was to be born anew. To be born anew is to be regenerated with the divine life, a life other than the human life received by natural birth. Hence, his real need was not better teachings, but the divine life. Nicodemus was seeking for teachings, which belong to the tree of knowledge, but the Lord's answer turned him to the need of life, which belongs to the tree of life (cf. Gen. 2:9-17). The Lord told Nicodemus very emphatically that what he needed was to be born again. Thus, man's real need is to be regenerated with another life. All of us must realize that what we need is not religion or teaching to regulate and correct us, but another life, the life of God, to regenerate us. Man needs regeneration because he needs the divine life. Regardless of how good you are, you still do not have the life of God. You need another birth in order to receive the life of God with His divine nature. Although you may feel that you are good, you must admit that you do not have the life of God with His divine nature. Another birth, regeneration, is necessary that you may receive another life, the divine life of God.

The Lord's answer to Nicodemus cut across his

human, traditional, religious concept. The Lord seemed to be telling Nicodemus, "Nicodemus, what you need is not teaching, but another life. Regardless of how good you are, you have only the human life. You need the divine life. Nicodemus, don't you realize that by seeking knowledge you are on the line of the tree of knowledge? You are not on the line of the tree of life." Nicodemus was not on the line that would lead him to the New Jerusalem, but on the line that would take him to the lake of fire. Nicodemus, however, did not know that he was partaking of the wrong tree.

B. Man's Real Need—To Be Born Anew

1. Not to Enter the Mother's Womb and Be Born Again

When Nicodemus heard that he had to be born anew, he thought that this meant that he had to go back to his mother's womb and come out again. His answer proves that he did not know how to exercise his spirit. He misunderstood the Lord's word. Then the Lord Jesus said that that which is born of the flesh is flesh. He seemed to be saying to Nicodemus, "Regardless of the number of times you go back into your mother's womb and come out again, you still will be flesh. That which is born of the flesh is flesh. Nicodemus, there is no need for you to say that you can't go back to your mother's womb and be born a second time, for even if you could do it, you would still be the same. Even if you could be born anew in that way and be young again, after another sixty or seventy years you would be the same as you are now. You do not need that kind of rebirth." Nicodemus did not need another birth in time, but another birth in nature.

2. *But to Be Born of Water and the Spirit*

"Jesus answered, Truly, truly, I say to you, Unless one is born of water and the Spirit, he cannot enter into the kingdom of God" (John 3:5). Water is the central sign of the ministry of John the Baptist, that is, to bury and terminate people of the old creation. In his ministry, John the Baptist came to baptize with water. He told people that they had to repent and realize that they were fallen and good for nothing except burial. Everyone who heard John's preaching and repented was baptized in water. This means that, as fallen men of the old creation, they were being terminated. That was John's ministry. Furthermore, John told people that his ministry was for the ministry of the Lord Jesus. As water is the central sign in the ministry of John the Baptist, Spirit is the central significance of the ministry of Jesus, that is, to germinate people in the new creation. These two main concepts, water and Spirit, when put together, are the whole concept of the matter of regeneration. Regeneration, to be born anew, is the termination of the people of the old creation with all their deeds, and their germination in the new creation with the divine life. What does it mean to be born again? It means to be terminated by John's ministry through water and to be germinated by Jesus' ministry through the Spirit.

How can we have the ministry of John the Baptist today? We have it by repentance. Whenever a person repents, confessing that he is a fallen being who is good for nothing, that is the acceptance of John's ministry. There is no need, of course, for John literally to be present, for his ministry is in the New Testament already. When we preach the gospel, we firstly preach the ministry of John. That is why we preach very much about sin and repentance. Whoever accepts this ministry, in one sense, is terminated, and, in another sense, is born of water. Following repentance, everyone must believe in the Lord Jesus and accept His ministry of life in order to be germinated. In order to accept salvation, we need both repentance and faith. To repent is to receive John's ministry, and to believe is to accept the ministry of the Lord Jesus. This is regeneration. Now we understand what it means to be born of water and of the Spirit.

The Lord made Nicodemus's situation very clear to him. Everyone, whether he is good or bad, needs to be terminated through water and then germinated with the divine life. This is the second birth, a birth not of the mother's womb, but of water and of the Spirit. [3]

THE WAY TO BE REGENERATED

What is the way for us to be regenerated? How can we receive regeneration? In verses 15, 16, 18, and 36, the Lord said, "That everyone who believes in Him may have eternal life"; "that everyone who believes in Him should not perish, but have eternal life"; "he who believes in Him is not judged"; "he who believes in the Son has eternal life." These emphatic words spoken repeatedly by the Lord tell us clearly and definitely that the way for us to be saved and regenerated is simply to believe in the Lord. To believe is the only way for us to receive salvation and regeneration. It is absolutely a matter of faith. Regardless of how much we can work or how good our work may be, we cannot be saved and regenerated by our work. Our work does not count in this matter. Only faith counts. Salvation and regeneration must be by faith. It is by faith in the Lord, by believing in the Lord, that we receive forgiveness, the release from God's condemnation negatively. It is also by faith, by believing in the Lord, that we receive eternal life, the divine life of God, positively for our regeneration. The Lord has accomplished the redemptive work for us. By His redemptive death on the cross, He has met all of God's righteous demands on us and has fulfilled all the requirements of God's righteousness, holiness, and glory for us. By His death on the cross in the form of the serpent, the Lord has even destroyed Satan, the devil who usurps us and enslaves us, that we might be delivered from the evil one's slavery and power of death (Heb. 2:14). All negative things have been solved by His all-inclusive death on the cross. We do not need to do anything except believe in what the Lord has accomplished. He has dealt with and solved all of our problems. He has left no room for our doing or work. So, there is no need of our work, only of faith in His finished, completed, and all-inclusive redemptive work.

After passing through death, by and in resurrection, the Lord has released His life and has become a life-giving Spirit (1 Cor. 15:45). Now, in resurrection, He is the Spirit of life (2 Cor. 3:17), with all the virtue of His redemptive work, waiting for us to believe in Him. Once we believe in Him, we not only receive the forgiveness of sins and the deliverance from Satan's evil power of darkness, but we also receive the Spirit of life, that is, the Lord Himself, with the eternal life of God. In this way we are saved and regenerated. It is by the way of believing in the Lord with His all-inclusive redemptive work that we receive God's life and are born of Him to be His sons.

THE WAY TO BELIEVE

To believe in the Lord means to receive Him (John 1:12). The Lord is receivable. He is now the life-giving Spirit, with His complete redemption, waiting for and expecting us to receive Him. Our spirit is the receiving organ. We can receive the Lord's Spirit into our spirit by believing in Him. Once we believe in Him, He, as the Spirit, enters into our spirit. Then we are regenerated by Him, the life-giving Spirit, and become one spirit with Him (1 Cor. 6:17). The phrase "believes in" in verses 16, 18, and 36 literally translated should be "believes into." When we believe in the Lord, we believe into Him. By believing in Him, we get into Him to be one with Him, to partake of Him, and to participate in all that He has accomplished for us. By believing into Him, we are identified with Him in all that He is and in all that He has passed through, accomplished, attained, and obtained. As we become one with Him by believing into Him, we are saved and regenerated by Him as life. It is by believing into Him that we partake of Him as life and are regenerated in Him. [4]

If you have not yet received the Lord into you, you can receive Him now. Please pray the following simple prayer:

"Lord Jesus! I am a sinner. I need You. Come into my spirit. Take away my sins. Fill me that I may have the life of God. I receive You right now as my Savior and life. I give myself to You. I ask this in Jesus' name. Amen!"

SOURCE

[1] *Life-study of John,* Message One, p. 13.
[2] *Life-study of John,* Message Two, p. 25.
[3] *Life-study of John,* Message Eight, pp. 91-102.
[4] *Life-study of John,* Message Nine, pp. 116-118.

By Witness Lee, published by Living Stream Ministry.

The Way to Experience God in the Gospel of John

THE WORD, THE FLESH, AND THE BREATH

In the Gospel of John, there are three wonderful words. In the first chapter, the first verse, we read, "In the beginning was the Word." So we have the *Word*. Then in the same chapter there is another word, *flesh*. "And the Word became flesh and tabernacled among us" (v. 14). Then at the end of the book, in chapter twenty, we have *breath*. Jesus, the resurrected One, breathed on the disciples and told them to receive the Holy Spirit (v. 22). "Spirit" in Greek means "breath." So, here it can be rendered "breath." He breathed upon the disciples and told them to receive the holy breath. So we have three words: the Word, the flesh, and the breath. The Word was God, the flesh is man, and the breath is the Spirit.

The Gospel of John is a wonderful book. In the beginning, in eternity, there was God who was the Word. But on the earth, in time, He became a man who was flesh. Then from chapter one to chapter twenty we see a man as the flesh who was the Lamb of God that took away the sin of the world (1:29). With Him there is incarnation, crucifixion (including redemption), resurrection, and ascension. Then eventually, He came back to the disciples to do simply one thing: to breathe on them and ask them to receive Him as the breath. This is the end of this book. In the beginning was the Word, and at the end is the breath. And in this breath everything is included.

Just consider again the whole Gospel of John. In the beginning was the Word and the Word was God, and the Word was made flesh to be the Lamb of God to take away the sin of the world. He accomplished redemption by crucifixion, and He was buried and resurrected. Did He become a great Lord to sit on the throne for man to bow down to worship Him? Is this in the Gospel of John? No! Jesus in the Gospel of John is not like this. In the beginning was the Word and the Word was made flesh, and eventually the flesh was resurrected to be the breath for us to breathe in.

CHRIST AS THE BREATH

Read the Gospel of John again. It is wonderful. In the beginning was the Word, the Word was made flesh, and the flesh was resurrected to become a breath. Then He came back to the disciples, not as a great giant asking everyone to bow down to worship Him, but in a very silent way. All of a sudden He was there, and nobody knew how He came in (20:19). He was just there. And He did not tell them to do this or to do that.

He did something rather unusual. He breathed on them. He simply breathed on them and told them to receive the holy breath. That is all.

He did not tell the disciples, "I am the Son of God, and I have been resurrected; so you must do this to glorify Me, and you must do that to magnify Me." He did not tell them to do anything. He just breathed on them and told them to receive the holy breath. That was good enough, because everything is included in that breath.

From that time He was never absent from them. He came, but He never left, because now He, as the holy breath, was within all the disciples. This is the Gospel of John. I am afraid most Christians know the beginning of John, but they are not clear about the ending of John.

The beginning of this book is something very high, very profound, and very great. "In the beginning was the Word and the Word…was God" (1:1). Everything that was made was made through Him, and in Him was life, and this life was the light of men (vv. 3-4). But at the end the disciples went fishing (21:3). And while they were fishing, this wonderful One also was there. Just compare the two ends of this book. The beginning is very high, but the ending seems very low.

But the secret, the mystery of Christ, is with these seemingly foolish ones. To them He was just like the breath. That is all. After all that He accomplished in this Gospel, He was just the breath. This is the third stage of Christ.

In the first stage He was God. In the second stage He was man as the Lamb of God to accomplish redemption. But in the third stage He is simply the breath. This is why it is rather hard for people to realize Him.

We all know Christ in the first and second stages, but we do not know Him properly and accurately in the third stage. You may say, "Well, I have heard that there is the Holy Spirit, and that Christ is in the Holy Spirit." You have heard this, but we must know more adequately that Christ is not only *in* the Spirit, but Christ *is* the Spirit. "And the Lord is the Spirit" (2 Cor. 3:17). He is the Spirit, the breath, the air. He is the life-giving Spirit (1 Cor. 15:45).

THE INDWELLING BREATH

If Christ were not the life-giving Spirit, who is as available as breath or air, how could He be in us? If Christ were not the spiritual breath, the heavenly air, how could He be our life? Christ is in the heavens, and we are on the earth. How could something in the heavens be our life? If anything is to be our life, it must be in us.

In the beginning of this Gospel we see the Word expressing and explaining God. But this Word was made flesh in order to accomplish redemption and remove all the barriers that God may come into man. Now He is not only the Word, but also the Word plus the flesh—God plus man.

But this is not all. He must come into man in order to be his life. How can He do this? There is no other way but to be resurrected and be made a life-giving Spirit, just like breath or air. The air fills the whole earth. Wherever we go, the air is waiting for us to breathe it in.

This is the Gospel of John. This book eventually brings us to the point of this wonderful Christ being so available, even like the air that we breathe. It is very easy for Him to get into us, because He is the air. Since He is the breath, we may simply breathe Him in. Now in this spiritual breath we have God, man, incarnation, crucifixion, resurrection, and ascension. Everything is included in this heavenly air. It is wonderful and so all-inclusive. [1]

THE WAY TO EXPERIENCE GOD

The way to experience God begins in John chapter four. In verse 24 the Lord said, "God is Spirit, and those who worship Him must worship in spirit and truthfulness." To worship God is to contact God, to enjoy God, and to partake of all He is. Worshipping God is a matter of taking God into us. It is not merely objective, but also subjective. This is proved by the fact that in this chapter the Lord speaks, on the one hand, about worship and, on the other hand, about drinking the living water (v. 14). If we put verses 14 and 24 together, we shall see that to drink of the living water is to worship God. Moreover, worshipping God by our spirit and in our spirit is the real drinking of the living water, which is God Himself. God Himself is the Spirit, and this Spirit is the living water. We drink this living water by worshipping God. Hence, drinking of God and worshipping Him are synonymous. We all must drink the very God, who is the living water, the Spirit.

Another aspect of the way is unveiled in chapter six. In verse 48 the Lord said, "I am the bread of life," and in verse 57 He said, "He who eats Me, he also shall live because of Me." The way is not only to drink God as the living water, but also to eat Christ, the embodiment of God, as the living bread. The Lord's word about eating Him was offensive to the religious people, and they could not bear it (v. 60). In verse 63 the Lord said to His disciples, "It is the Spirit who gives life; the flesh profits nothing; the words which I have spoken to you are spirit and are life." The Lord seemed to be saying, "I am the bread of life. But I can be dispensed into you as your life supply only through the living Word. This living Word is the Spirit." Thus, we must not contact the living Word as the black and white letters; we must contact the living Word as the living Spirit by exercising our spirit. Thus, the way to experience Christ is to contact the very God, who is the Spirit, and to eat and drink of Him.

THE OVERFLOW

If we truly contact the Lord and eat and drink

of Him, we shall have the overflow spoken of in 7:37 and 38. On the last day of the Feast of Tabernacles Jesus stood and cried out, saying, "If anyone thirsts, let him come to Me and drink. He who believes into Me, as the Scripture said, out of his innermost being shall flow rivers of living water." What an overflow! Whoever believes in Him will have an overflow of rivers of living water. The water the believers take in of Christ will become overflowing rivers.

If you have such an overflow, could you help but love the Lord? Could you still live in sin and continue to love the world? This would be impossible. There is no need to strive to overcome sin and the world. There is not even any need to try to love the Lord. In fact, there is no need for us to do anything. Because we realize that the Triune God has been wrought into our being, and that we have been constituted with His riches and have become parts of Him, something naturally and spontaneously will flow out of us. [2]

DRINKING, EATING, AND BREATHING

If we consider these various items covered in John, we realize how vital they are for our existence. Without drinking, eating, and breathing we could not live.

These three means for our physical existence are all used by the Lord Jesus to illustrate how we may take Him. He is our water, more refreshing than the best earthly drink. We must drink Him!

He is our bread. We must eat Him! Bread is not merely to be looked at. Its purpose is to be eaten. Christ as the living bread must be eaten. Do not think that to say this is uncultured and wild. He says Himself that we must eat Him.

He is our breath, imparting Himself as life to us. We must breathe Him!

This enjoyment of Jesus is God's economy. It is this that He would recover among His people. Jesus is the living water, the living bread, and the living breath. We must drink of Him, eat Him, and breathe Him.

THE WAY TO TAKE CHRIST IN

There are two ways by which we may drink, eat, and breathe Jesus. These are the Word and the Spirit. "It is the Spirit who gives life; the words which I have spoken to you are spirit and are life" (John 6:63). This verse mentions both the Word and the Spirit. The very Word revealed in John 1:1 eventually became the Spirit. It is this Spirit who is the water, the bread, and the breath.

John 20:22 reads, "Receive the Holy *pneuma*." This Greek word *pneuma* may be translated either as "spirit" or as "breath." It is equally correct to say, "Receive the Holy Spirit" or "Receive the holy breath." The Spirit today is our breath. This breath is Jesus, the incarnate Word who went to the cross, entered into resurrection, and ascended to the heavens. He then returned to us as the life-giving Spirit.

We have the Word outside us and the Spirit inside us. Day by day we must come to the Word, not only with our mind but also with our heart and spirit. As we open the Bible, we must open our whole being. We must read not only with our understanding but also with prayer. The Bible is not an ordinary book. In this holy Word there is life, the Spirit, God, and Jesus Christ. These are all contained in the Word and are conveyed to us as we open ourselves and pray. This prayerful reading of the Word is the eating, drinking, and breathing in of the Lord.

How would you answer if someone asked you where God is? Do not say that God is in the heavens. Heaven is too far away. How could one get there to find Him? God, you must tell him, is in the Bible. Where is Christ? He too is in the Word. Where is the Spirit? Where is life? The answer to these questions is also "in the Word."

SPENDING TIME IN THE WORD

Spend time with this book. Besides your ten minutes in the morning, take a few more minutes at noon, and a few more in the evening. As you open this book, open yourself also. Read, understand, and pray. As you pray, you are drinking the water, eating the food, and breathing the air. You will grow. The more you take Christ into you in this way, the more Christ you will have growing in you. You will become another person. Do not expect quick results; growth takes time. It does not come about from a few concentrated days of praying and fasting and then having something fall upon you from the heavens. Take time to water the little seed of life sown into the soil of your heart. Not only will you grow; the church will also grow and be built up in this way. In the church meetings Christ will come forth in the teaching, the preaching, and the testifying. Such riches in the church life will convince and attract new ones.

REGULAR GROWTH

Do not be concerned about how much you understand of what you read. What matters is that you faithfully open the Word, open yourself, and read and pray. This is not a once-for-all procedure. It is not like being born, but like breathing. Growth, like breathing, is continual, day by day and even minute by minute. You will grow by coming regularly to the Word. Carry a pocket version of the Word with you. Wherever you are, when you have a few minutes, open it and read a chapter or so, then pray over what you have read. There is little need for you to pray over your grades at school, or for your business to be successful, or for guidance when you go shopping. Simply pray the Word. In this way you will receive and enjoy God Himself.

PRAYING THE WORD

What do you think makes you healthy and strong? It is by eating, drinking, and breathing.

When it gets close to meal time you probably feel weak; you need to eat to regain your energy. The same is true spiritually. You are weak if you have not been eating, drinking, and breathing Christ in the Word. In fact, it is a mercy that you are still here. Do not try to run the race without food, drink, and air any longer! Come to the Word. Open to the Lord. Speak to Him the words you read. For example, you may pray the words of John 1:14 and 16: "The Word became flesh and tabernacled among us. Lord, thank You, You are the Word. You became flesh. Thank You that You tabernacled among us. Among us! Amen. Full of grace. Hallelujah, grace! Grace and reality. Amen, grace and reality! Of His fullness we have all received. We have all received. We have received, Lord, and we are receiving even now. Praise the Lord!" Does praying the Word in this way seem like foolishness to you? I tell you, it is the way to eat, drink, and breathe Christ. This is how we can live Christ, rather than living morality or ethics. Read and pray the Word![3]

SOURCE

[1] *The Stream,* pp. 20-22.
[2] *Life-study of John,* Message Fifty-one, pp. 609-612.
[3] *Life Messages,* pp. 22-26.

By Witness Lee, published by Living Stream Ministry.

OTHER BOOKS PUBLISHED BY
Living Stream Ministry

Titles by Witness Lee:

Titles by Watchman Nee:

Available at

Christian bookstores, or contact Living Stream Ministry
2431 W. La Palma Ave. • Anaheim, CA 92801
1-800-549-5164 • www.livingstream.com